SECRET
TO DOING
— THE —
RIGHT
THING

...When It Matters Most

Discover and Trust
Your *Inner Voice*

A Practical Guide to Living Without Regrets

HENRYK DETER

The Secret to Doing the Right Thing … When It Matters Most.
Discover and Trust Your Inner Voice.
A Practical Guide to Living Without Regrets.

ISBN: 978-3-911652-01-8

Acknowledgments

I'd like to express my heartfelt gratitude to the friends who supported me tirelessly with their feedback, offering invaluable insights that elevated the text, structure, and title beyond my initial draft: Carina, Ed, Marc, Mesa, Patric, and Tino (in alphabetical order).

Special thanks to another Marc, an accomplished author himself, who not only inspired me to embark on writing this book but also generously shared his wisdom through his works and our personal exchanges. His guidance and practical tips were instrumental in bringing this project to life, and I am deeply grateful for his encouragement and example.

Who I Am and Why I Wrote This Book

You might be wondering, "Why should I listen to this guy? What qualifies him to give me advice on something as personal as the inner voice and how to follow it?" Let me give you a bit of background.

I have spent my professional life in the business world, where I also engaged in co-authoring and co-publishing several books on practical, hard-nosed business topics. These were rooted in my nearly twenty-five-year-long consulting career, focused on making our company more successful and helping others improve their businesses. During that time, I also co-founded a small publishing house to market these books. Yet these weren't the kind of books that touch your heart—they were all about KPIs, data, strategies, and profits.

My professional career has been filled with goals, achievements, and responsibilities. Over time, though, I felt myself slipping further and further away from a sense of fulfillment.

Something was missing. Without a stable private situation during and after my divorce, I had lost touch with that part of me that listens to the gentle guidance of the inner voice, that deep knowing of what truly matters in life. This phase of my life ended in a deep personal crisis and burnout.

So, what led me to writing this book? Well, I've spent years learning, reflecting, and experiencing what it means to ignore your inner voice—and the price you pay when you do. My burnout and personal crisis were the wake-up calls that forced me to really listen. Since then, I've devoted myself to understanding not just my own journey, but the nature of the inner voice itself.

Over time, I've read extensively, attended seminars, and pulled together lessons from various fields—psychology, neuroscience, philosophy, and mindfulness practices.

My aim with this book is to distill what I've learned from all these sources, along with my own life experiences, into one guide that can help you reconnect with your inner wisdom. Think of this book as the best of the best: a handy guide that saves you the time and energy of piecing it together yourself. Think of me as being an expert, guide, and friend.

When I tell you about my life in this book, it is not because I think I am more important than anyone else. It is only so that you understand how I felt at various points in my life. Perhaps you can relate to it as you might see parallels to your life and learn something from my experiences. Maybe you also see differences because you are younger or older than me, have a different gender, come from a different part of the world, or because your life has simply taken a completely different professional or family path than mine. That doesn't matter at all, because I am firmly convinced and have experienced that we are all the same when it comes to certain topics—and that includes the topic of this book: the inner voice.

As an advisor, coach, and author, my aim is to help you harness the power of your own inner voice. I've faced doubt, taken wrong turns, and ultimately found my way back to myself. If my experiences can inspire or guide you to make better decisions and lead a more fulfilling life, then I've achieved my goal with this book.

Thank you for trusting me on this journey. I'm also very interested in hearing your story! Where are you in your life right now, and how has my book helped you connect with your inner voice and make the right choices for yourself?

Feel free to reach out via email at *books@henrykdeter.com*; I will personally respond.

As you read this book, remember—my ultimate goal is not for you to listen to me, but for you to listen to yourself.

Table of Contents

Chapter I. A Wake-Up Call in the Dark 1

Chapter II. It's Okay to Do Nothing: The Power of Your
Own Decision 7

Chapter III. From Rush Hour to Burnout: My Journey
Through Midlife and Beyond 11

Exercise 1. Timeline of Your Life 19

Chapter IV. Silencing the Saboteur: How to Tame Your
Inner Critic 23

Exercise 2. The Inner Critic Dialogue Protocol 29

Chapter V. The Gentle Whisper: Rediscovering the Voice
That Knows You Best 33

Exercise 3. Connect with Your Inner Voice Through Body
Awareness 51

Chapter VI. The Price of Ignoring Your Inner Voice............... 55

Exercise 4 Return to the Inner Truth............................. 69

Chapter VII. The Hidden Forces Behind Ignoring Your
    Inner Voice.. 71

Exercise 5. The Inner Resistance—Recognize and
    Overcome It... 77

Chapter VIII. Reconnecting with Your Inner Voice:
    Techniques to Find Your Center................................. 79

Exercise 6. Strengthening Self-awareness—Body and
    Behavior as a Mirror of the Inner Voice 105

Chapter IX. How to Tell If Your Inner Voice is Helping or
    Hurting You.. 109

Exercise 7. The Inner Voice Debate............................. 119

Chapter X. The Wisdom of Looking Back – Times Our
    Inner Voice Guided Us Well....................................... 123

Exercise 8. Reflecting on When Your Inner Voice Led You
    to Good Choices 139

Chapter XI. Head, Heart, or Gut: How We Process Our
Inner Voice..143

Exercise 9. What type are you? 151

Chapter XII. Your Next Big Move................................155

Exercise 10. The Wisdom of Your Inner Voice— What
Should I Change in My Life?.......................................157

Chapter XIII. The Final Step: Trusting and Acting on Your
Inner Voice..163

My Book Recommendations.......................................171

Chapter I

A Wake-Up Call in the Dark

It was summer. I wasn't feeling well. For some time, I'd had the feeling that I was only in my head. Only thinking, no more feeling. No inner compass anymore, no gut to guide me. Just functioning. I slept very badly during this time and was often irritable. I couldn't get excited about anything anymore. I found myself having more glasses of wine after work than I knew was healthy, using them as a way to unwind, quiet my thoughts, and seek some sense of relaxation. Everything that used to come easily to me in my job required an extreme amount of energy. I made more mistakes than usual, forgot things, canceled meetings because I could hardly motivate myself or simply no longer felt up to them. I then blamed it on feeling unwell or having a cold.

I wondered what was going on. A voice inside me always said something like: "Don't be like that. You're the boss, you have employees, customers, a business partner. You have to persevere and live up to your responsibilities. It'll get better, you're having a bit of a slump at the moment. You can't show weakness now. It's always worked before. Hang in there for a few more years, you can do it. Work is work and doesn't always have to be fun. You have to earn money, pay off your house, look after your children and save for your retirement."

My battery was almost completely flat. I saved myself for the summer vacations, two weeks to switch off with my two teenage children (I was newly divorced at the time, which had also taken a lot of energy and left clear scars). I was already familiar with this pattern existing over many years before: there would be a lot going on at work, I would be increasingly exhausted and long for a break. Then would come a nice summer vacation and afterwards my battery would be recharged. I'd be energized again, everything would feel exciting, and I'd truly enjoy my diverse consulting work—a role where, as a long-standing member and co-owner, I've had the privilege to help shape the direction and success of the company over many years.

This time was different. The vacation was great, with time with the kids, city trips, beach, good food, and staying in bed late in the mornings. At the same time, I realized that I couldn't really enjoy it. I read books to distract myself. I didn't read emails from work. Yet there was always a black cloud over me that constantly accompanied me. I couldn't interpret it and told myself again: "You're fine, stop making such a big deal out of it. You'll be okay!"

In the first week of work after the vacation, I noticed something that I had never experienced before: I wasn't recovered at all. I felt worse than before the vacation. The battery hadn't become fuller, but emptier. Or was it broken? Every meeting, every phone call, every email, simply everything at work was torture. I felt completely out of place. It was as if I were standing outside myself, watching everything from that position. I couldn't interpret it; I didn't understand it. I was now feeling very bad, I regularly consumed too much wine in the evenings after work to get my mind off things, and my sleep became increasingly poor. Then, on the weekend after this first week of work after the vacation, I suddenly regained some clarity.

I heard my inner voice. It had probably been talking to me for a long time, but I couldn't or didn't want to hear it until then. Suddenly I heard it. Probably because it had been screaming so loudly that even a deaf person couldn't have missed it anymore. It shouted, "STOP. THIS. NOW!"

I knew immediately that I had to listen to this inner voice, as otherwise things wouldn't turn out well for me. First thing Monday morning, I spoke to my long-time friend and business partner, with whom I had run our company for many years, and opened up to him: "I'm not feeling well. I need a break."

At that point, I was approaching my fiftieth birthday, just six weeks away, after spending over twenty-two years at the company, much of that time as a board member and shareholder. It had always been unthinkable for me to ever leave this company prematurely. The break eventually turned out to be a state of complete mental exhaustion, commonly known as "burnout".

Slowly and gradually, I recovered, sought help, did things that were good for me and spent a lot of time thinking about the question: What is wrong with me? How could it get this far? And how can I get out of it? What's the next step in my life? I'd always thought of myself as a resilient person who went through life in a reflective way, who had his activities and downtime outside of work, and thought about the important questions in life.

Five months after starting my "break", I told my partner that I would not be returning. This was both the most difficult and the most important step I have ever taken at one of the most important crossroads in my life.

The secret to doing the right thing, when it mattered most, lay in listening to what my inner voice was urging me to do. It had become a decision between holding on and letting go of what no longer felt right.

Since then, I have been intensively occupied with the question of what kind of voice it was (or was it several voices?) that first steered me in the wrong direction and then (probably just in time) in the right direction?

With this book, I would like to share my experience and knowledge with you, so that you don't get to this point in the first place. Or, if you do, so that you can get out of it as well as I did.

In my case, the shift was dramatic, a clear-cut break from a career that had defined me for more than two decades. For you, however, the right decision doesn't need to be as drastic; whether it's a major life change or a subtle realignment, your inner voice will guide you to the path that suits your unique journey.

Chapter II

It's Okay to Do Nothing:
The Power of Your Own Decision

Before we really get started, let me briefly explain to you the structure of the book: I will guide you step by step in dealing with your own inner voice. For this purpose, I will always tell you a little about my own experience, so you may recognize parallels in your life. At the end of each chapter, you'll find a practical exercise that lets you apply the chapter's ideas in a hands-on way. There are ten exercises in total, each requiring a bit of time and a quiet space. If you're planning to read through the book quickly, you might want to familiarize yourself with the exercises first and come back to them later.

However, it would be a shame if you didn't do the exercises at all, because on a purely theoretical level, it will be difficult or even impossible to find your way to yourself and your inner voice.

Or to put it positively: if you read this book and seriously try out the exercises contained in each chapter, I am sure you will encounter your inner voice.

It is not unlikely though, that it will confront you with uncomfortable truths, because we all tend to bury emotions, avoid difficult decisions, or ignore aspects of ourselves that we're afraid to face. I can understand if you now say: I have a bit of respect for that. What am I going to do with this new insight? Do I have to turn my life upside down? I don't know if I'm ready for that.

I can reassure you for two reasons. Firstly, these thoughts are completely normal. Most of us are reluctant to delve too deeply into ourselves for fear of uncovering skeletons in the closet. Unfortunately, personal growth usually takes place exactly where it becomes uncomfortable. You probably know that yourself, otherwise you wouldn't be reading this book. Secondly—and this is the best part—by the end of this book, I'll share a "one-million-dollar tip" on how to handle the insights you gain along the way. There is one option you have: do nothing! Everything stays as it is. You won't even feel bad about it. If you are already so curious and want to know how this works, secretly turn to chapter XIII of this book, where I will explain it to you. If you want to be surprised: thank you! Thank you for trusting me to take you on this little journey to yourself. It was very rewarding for me and I sincerely hope it will be for you, too.

Chapter III

From Rush Hour to Burnout:
My Journey Through Midlife and Beyond

Looking back, the first fifty-one years of my life flew by. This is probably true for pretty much all people in their thirties, forties, fifties, sixties ... who are at some point asking themselves how the "rest" of their lives should go.

I started a little later than most in both my career and family life, taking my time before diving into adulthood's more serious commitments. The first degree I pursued after high school and civil service didn't feel like the right fit. At twenty-two, I spent a transformative year in Florida, and afterward, I found my ideal path: a degree in International Business Administration, which included foreign languages and semesters abroad in the Midwest of the US and in

Mexico. I was twenty-seven years old when I started my first serious full-time job. At thirty-four, I bought into the company and joined the executive board. As you already know, at the age of almost fifty, I then slid into burnout, while still working for that same company.

As for my family life, I met my future wife at the age of twenty-five and we married when I was almost thirty-two. Our son joined us when I had just turned thirty-four, followed by his sister a little under two years after that. We moved about every five years, each time to a bigger and nicer apartment, and later to a house to rent. When I was forty-four, we bought our own house for the first time and renovated it extensively before moving in.

Despite some setbacks and hardships that life inevitably brings—deaths and serious illnesses in the family and among friends, my own severe accident at the age of twenty-four, etc.—I was doing well. Things were generally always moving upward. All the things that I could never really imagine as a young person, both professionally and privately, were there at some point. I worked a lot, but I liked it and I earned well.

We could afford everything we needed and went on great trips.

The Rush Hour of Life: Balancing Responsibility

Looking back, I realize that from my late twenties to mid-thirties, I steadily took on more responsibilities—for my wife, my children, my business partner, employees, and clients. Eventually, this extended to my parents and brother, whom I supported in various ways. I welcomed these responsibilities, felt at ease with them, and managed to carry the weight comfortably for quite some time.

This phase is often referred to as the "rush hour of life" for good reason—just like the real rush hour during evening traffic in a big city, for several years, all the major areas of life are active at the same time and everything feels like it's operating at full capacity. There is little or no time to think, to catch our breath, to really reflect. We are predominantly in performance mode, in hustle mode, and have to function, i.e., fulfill our various responsibilities.

For me, it was the case that I didn't question much over the years. I accepted things as being just the way life is. Your own life sometimes takes a back seat. There's also little room for the romantic, emotional part of the partnership. It's all about "taking care". It's about "we have to do this; we have to do that". I largely accepted this as the course of life. At the same time, I realized that I was going through a full-blown midlife crisis. Even though I was often very grateful for my family, my great healthy children, my exciting and lucrative job— nothing was like it used to be.

Midlife Crisis: The Heaviest Burden

I no longer felt carefree, and was less spontaneous, less flexible, and laughed less. I had little attention for, or mindfulness of, the little beauties, moments of happiness, and wonders of life. The burden I was carrying felt heavier and heavier, threatening to crush me. Back and neck pain were my physical symptoms, which in a figurative sense stemmed from the constant heavy load on my shoulders.

At the same time, a lot was simply *there* now. As a young person, I started out with very little, had nothing to lose, and the world was open to me. Everything that happened then happened for the first time. It was exciting and involved a lot of personal growth. At some point, I felt I'd reached a personal plateau. I couldn't go any further *upwards*; rather, I was latently afraid of falling off this plateau over the edge.

I know that I am anything but alone in this. The phenomenon of the midlife crisis has been sufficiently described, but was always a bit too simple an explanation for me—until I read about scientific research into the U-curve of happiness.

The U-Curve of Happiness: Scientific Insights

Research into the U-curve of happiness can be traced back to several scientists and studies, with economist Andrew Oswald from the University of Warwick in England, and US economist David G. Blanchflower, playing a central role. Their studies have confirmed the existence of the U-curve in many different countries and cultures. They analyzed extensive survey data and found that people's subjective perception of happiness is highest in early adulthood, between the ages of eighteen and thirty. In this phase, people are often more optimistic, still have many future expectations, and experience greater freedom with fewer obligations. From then on, however, happiness goes downhill. Statistically speaking, the low point of the U-curve of happiness for many people is between the ages of 45-50. Studies show that this is the age at which well-being is often at its lowest. After this, happiness levels tend to rise again and the second peak tends to occur at an older age, often from around sixty or even later. People in this stage of life often report greater satisfaction because they have less stress and responsibility and view life from a more relaxed perspective. In addition, many older people place more value on the here and now and are increasingly less concerned about their own future.

Reflecting on Life: Listening to the Inner Voice

In my opinion, these phases of life are also strongly influenced by how much people are *with themselves*. And also, how well they can hear their inner voice and act accordingly.

Which brings us to the subject of this book. Why am I telling you my life story? On one hand, because in retrospect it has contributed a lot to the fact that I didn't hear my inner voice for so long and would have driven head-on into a wall at high speed if my inner voice hadn't made me pull over in time. Secondly, I would like to encourage you to think about your life story: how can you divide up and describe the phases of your life? How did you feel during them? Where are you today? To do this, I would like to ask you to practice the first exercise in this book.

Exercise 1

Timeline of Your Life

Goal of the Exercise

Visualize the significant changes in your life and understand how they have influenced your happiness and overall well-being. Reflect on the strategies you've used to cope with these changes and how they have impacted your personal growth.

Materials

- A large sheet of paper
- A pen or marker
- Optionally, different colors to highlight positive and negative events more clearly

Instructions

Step 1. Draw Your Life Line

- Lay the sheet of paper horizontally on the table.

- Draw a horizontal line across the entire sheet—this represents the course of your life, with your age on the X-axis (from childhood on the left to your current age on the right).

- This will act as your baseline, representing neutral emotions.

Step 2. Mark Significant Life Events

- Think about key life events that have had an impact on you. These could be related to your career, personal life, health, or emotional experiences.

- Mark these events along the horizontal line at the corresponding age or life stage when they occurred.

Step 3. Draw Highs and Lows

- For each life event, visualize how it affected your happiness and emotional well-being by drawing a curve that rises above the baseline for positive moments and dips below it for negative experiences.

20

- The height of the curve should reflect how happy or fulfilled you felt during that time (the higher the curve, the greater the happiness), while lows indicate difficult or challenging times (the lower the dip, the more challenging the experience).

- Connect these highs and lows to create a continuous curve that illustrates the emotional journey of your life.

Step 4. Reflect on Your Timeline

Look at your completed timeline and reflect on the following:

- Where do you see the most significant highs and lows?

- How did you handle challenging periods, and what helped you get through them?

- Do you notice any patterns? For example, did you consistently recover from lows and find your way back to positive experiences?

- Are there any gaps between your external circumstances and how you felt internally at those times?

Step 5. Identify Key Insights

- After reflecting, write down three key insights you've gained from analyzing your timeline:

- What lessons can you apply to future changes in your life?

- Is there anything you wish to let go of in order to be more open to happiness and growth?

Chapter IV

Silencing the Saboteur:
How to Tame Your Inner Critic

In this book, I would like to bring you closer to your inner voice again. Perhaps you are now saying:

"I still don't quite understand what you mean. My inner voice is already talking to me all the time. Even in the evening, when I actually want to go to sleep. And especially at night, when I wake up, the thoughts in my head immediately start spinning. They tell me what I have to do the next day or remind me of who I was annoyed with the day before. I also think about what I would have liked to say to that person but wasn't quick-witted enough to say at that moment."

That is *not* the inner voice I'm referring to—the one you're trying to reconnect with.

The Science Behind Self-Sabotage

What you're describing is more of the mental chatter, often dominated by self-criticism and worry, rather than guidance. Blair Singer captures this distinction well in his book *Little Voice Mastery*. Singer, a business trainer, speaker, and entrepreneur from the US, describes this critical inner dialogue as the *little voice*. This voice feeds on self-doubt, fear, and limiting beliefs, often sabotaging us just when we're faced with big challenges. It says things like "You can't do it!" or "What if you fail?", draining our energy, focus, and motivation.

This inner critic has also been thoroughly researched within the framework of cognitive behavioral therapy (CBT). In CBT, negative thoughts and dysfunctional beliefs are seen as the primary drivers of the sabotaging inner voice. These thoughts are often automated and take the form of cognitive distortions, such as catastrophizing ("I will fail.") or black-and-white thinking ("If it's not perfect, it's a failure."). Albert Ellis and Aaron Beck, two American psychiatrists, psychologists, and psychotherapists who are the pioneers of CBT, show that we are often controlled by irrational beliefs that form the basis for the inner critic. These beliefs, e.g., "I have to be perfect." or "I'm not good enough.", lead us to sabotage ourselves.

This rational, often an overly critical part of our thinking, determines the whole day for most of us—and often half the night too. In the months leading up to my burnout, I felt like I was operating entirely in my head, and nowhere else. I could vividly feel how my head was almost running hot like a battery from which too much power was being tapped at once. My nervous system, which is responsible for transmitting signals in the brain, was also permanently tense, almost in a state of emergency.

In behavioral therapy, the origin of these destructive thoughts is often traced back to earlier life experiences, particularly childhood experiences. These experiences shape how we perceive the world and ourselves. Negative beliefs often arise from critical or negative feedback that we have received from important caregivers (parents, teachers, friends). Social norms and past failures also shape our thinking. The inner critic is often seen as a protective mechanism designed to shield us from danger. Through self-criticism, the brain tries to motivate us not to break these social norms or repeat mistakes, and to be successful in social or professional situations. However, this mechanism can become dysfunctional if self-criticism becomes excessive and impairs our ability to develop positively and constructively.

These limiting beliefs often manifest themselves as automatic thoughts that pop up in a flash without us consciously realizing them. There is therefore a great danger that we confuse them with the inner voice that I tell you about in this book. In chapter IX, I'll show you how to (re)learn to distinguish this sabotaging inner voice from the supportive one.

The Power of Negative Thought Patterns

In a mindfulness course that I took during my burnout phase, I heard astonishing figures about our thoughts, which I later verified. They blew my mind! Here they are.

Researchers assume that the average person has around 60,000 to 70,000 thoughts per day. This figure comes from various psychological studies, but can certainly only be a rough estimate, intended to illustrate the high number of mental processes that our brain goes through every day.

It is estimated that around 95% (you heard right: ninety-five) of the thoughts we think every day are repetitive, i.e., thoughts that we have thought before. This means that only a very small proportion of our thoughts are really new or original. This is because our brain tends to fall back on familiar thought patterns and routines. In other words: we spend 95% of our waking lives more or less going round in circles.

What is really frightening is that around 80% of the thoughts we have every day are said to be negative. This figure underlines the extent to which our thinking can be characterized by self-doubt, fears, and negative expectations. These negative thoughts can take the form of worry, self-criticism, or pessimistic expectations.

As already mentioned, cognitive behavioral therapy assumes that many of our thoughts are automatic, especially the negative ones. This means that we often fall into negative thought patterns without conscious control, which are repeated in our daily thinking. We are then on autopilot. I was trapped in this state for a long time, no longer really acting but only reacting or running an automatic program.

Of course, these figures are generalizations. The exact number of thoughts and their quality can vary greatly from person to person and depend on their life situation. However, I personally have no doubt that this was exactly the case for me for quite some time, until I gradually found myself and my inner voice again.

Moving Beyond the Critic: Steps to Reclaim Your Inner Voice

Before we get to know the benevolent, helpful inner voice better in the rest of this book, and also talk about how to distinguish the critical from the benevolent inner voice, I would like you to deal with the saboteur within you a little. If you get to know your enemy, you can deal with him more calmly and disarm him to a certain extent (actually he is not your enemy at all and only wants to help you—but unfortunately, he often overdoes it. This can be explained by evolution, which I will come to later in this book.).

Exercise 2

The Inner Critic Dialogue Protocol

Goal of the Exercise

This exercise aims to help you better understand your inner critic and identify negative beliefs that may be holding you back. It involves three steps: observe, identify, and reformulate. By engaging in this practice, you will unmask your inner critic, recognize limiting beliefs, and gradually replace them with more constructive, positive thoughts. With consistent effort, you can learn to disarm the critical voice and shift your focus to the supportive, benevolent inner voice that empowers and strengthens you.

Instructions

Step 1. Observe—the inner critic in action

- Sit down in a quiet environment where you are undisturbed. Close your eyes and take a few deep breaths to relax.

29

- Recall a situation where you felt criticized or unsure of yourself. This could be a recent situation or something from the past.

- Listen to the thoughts that came up in this situation. What exactly did your inner critic say to you? Try to repeat these thoughts in your head as literally as possible.

- Write down the thoughts you have observed without judging them. Write down each critical thought as precisely as possible.

Step 2. Identify—recognize negative beliefs

- Look carefully at the thoughts you have written down and ask yourself for each one: "What do I believe underlies these thoughts?"

- Try to identify the limiting beliefs that are causing these thoughts. These could be beliefs such as "I am not good enough.", "I have to be perfect.", or "I will always fail.".

- Write down the identified beliefs. It can be helpful to start each belief with "I believe that ..." to make it clear to you that it is a belief that does not necessarily correspond to reality.

Step 3. Rephrasing—disarming the inner critic

- Select one of the identified negative beliefs and ask yourself: "Is this really true? Is there any evidence to prove the opposite?"

- Formulate a more positive, helpful belief based on your insights. For example, "I'm not good enough." could be rephrased as "I have strengths and weaknesses like everyone else, and I'm working to improve.".

- Write the new, positive belief next to the original belief. Repeat this new sentence a few times out loud or in your mind to internalize it.

Completion of the exercise

- Reflection: Take a few minutes to think about how the new beliefs make you feel. Do you feel lighter or less burdened? If so, make a note of this change.

- Tip: Repeat this exercise regularly to gradually identify and reformulate any limiting beliefs that are weighing you down.

Chapter V

The Gentle Whisper: Rediscovering the Voice That Knows You Best

In the last chapter, you dealt with the inner critic that may often get in your way and make your life difficult. You know yourself that this is not the inner voice that is taking you forward and that you are currently searching for. You want to reconnect with the good, the helpful, the benevolent inner voice. It helps you to make difficult, groundbreaking decisions in your life. It speaks when you are trying to choose the right educational path, a stay abroad, the choice of career or employer, a romantic relationship, the decision to bring children into the world, or anything else that is really important to you. It can also support you in more everyday situations (and often does so without you always realizing it). But what kind of voice is it? Where does this voice originate and *who* is actually speaking to you?

A Life-Changing Crisis: Listening to My Inner Voice

When I was turning fifty and going through my severe personal crisis and total exhaustion, which ultimately led to me leaving my own business after almost twenty-three years and starting something completely new (such as writing this book), my inner voice guided me twice.

Firstly, it did so in the moment when I made an oath of disclosure to my business partner on a Monday morning, a week after the summer vacations. I told him the realization that had dawned on me over the weekend: "I'm not well. I can't take any more. I need a break!" How did I know? Well, because by then I truly felt awful. I was desperate, having realized for quite some time that this job no longer brought me any joy and I was just going through the motions. My partner's initial reaction was great. He could clearly see that I was really not well and he *prescribed* that I should take four weeks off work and then we would see. I was very grateful to him and a huge burden was lifted. At the same time, I knew immediately that four weeks would not be enough to get me out of this state.

Back then I couldn't see a way out of my misery, as I was heavily involved in the company and felt an obligation and responsibility to my partner, my employees, and my customers. My business partner and I had known each other since we were teenagers. We met at the sports club in our hometown of Frankfurt in Germany, playing table tennis together. We had been through many ups and downs together over the years. Our friendship took a back seat though when we were busy building and running the company together. Our characters and skills complemented each other perfectly. However, since I played a very central role in the day-to-day operations, I was very afraid of letting him down and I simply couldn't imagine letting him continue on his own.

Of course, I also felt an obligation and responsibility to my family, as I had the role of provider in various ways. That weekend, I heard my inner voice louder than ever before. My head was practically throbbing as it screamed at me: "STOP THIS IMMEDIATELY! GET OUT OF THERE OR IT WILL END BADLY FOR YOU!". Today, I realize that it had been speaking to me for quite some time, kindly, under-standingly, and patiently—but also firmly and insistently when needed. I just didn't listen because I didn't want to— and probably couldn't at the time.

A Second Turning Point: Finding Clarity in Silence

The second time my inner voice helped me to make a fundamental decision was a few months later. I used my time out to recover, shifted down several gears, had professional therapeutic talks, got to know the concept of mindfulness-based stress reduction with regular meditation, went on a few short recovery vacations to get a change of scenery, read a lot and listened to podcasts about my problem, and went hiking. During this time, I realized that simply stepping away from the constant stress and rigid structure of my workday allowed me to reconnect with both my inner self and the world around me. I heard the birds chirping and streams rushing, smelled nature, and enjoyed sunrises and sunsets. I became present for things that I hadn't even noticed before my breakdown. At the beginning of my time out, I was still convinced that I would return to the old company after a period of recovery and keep going for a few more years. At the same time, I didn't want to set a fixed date for this, as even the thought of it caused me stress, putting me almost in a panic. So, I gave myself time and waited to see what would happen inside me. Wouldn't you know it, I felt better and better, gradually enjoying life again, especially the little things such as going for a walk, grocery shopping, or cooking lunch for my children.

I also got back in touch with myself. I was able to deal with my thoughts more constructively and increasingly got back into the driver's seat of my thinking. I learned to appreciate and practice the beautiful phrase: *Don't believe everything you think!* Because *thoughts are just thoughts.* I realized again that I have feelings. Yes, in retrospect that sounds very strange to me too, but during my difficult time I felt nothing. I exactly remember one of my meditation exercises. I was already a little advanced and had already practiced several, even longer sessions in silence. The voice on the tape instructed me to pay attention to my breathing, then gradually to pay attention first to my outside world and the sounds, then to my thoughts, my body awareness, and finally to my feelings. It wasn't about evaluating these perceptions, but simply perceiving them for what they are. And suddenly I felt something. I couldn't say then and I still can't say now what the feeling was. Was I happy or content, grateful or euphoric, at peace with myself, or simply very relaxed? I didn't care at all. I had a feeling that I couldn't put my finger on, but it felt great because it was a feeling, and a very strong one at that.

I made further progress on this journey back to myself and *listened* to myself. I had the vague certainty that the answers were within me, I just had to give them time. And so, I gave my benevolent inner voice the opportunity to speak to me. And what did it tell me? It reminded me of all the things I still wanted to do in my life, and how I wanted to live in the future. Again and again, the feeling of freedom, independence, and *being with myself* was very strong. I didn't want to go back to the dependencies I was subject to as an entrepreneur and board member of a consulting firm—back to my golden handcuffs. I paid attention to what my inner voice was telling me about my job in a completely non-judgmental and open way. It was amazing; not once did it tell me, "This is the right thing for you! You still enjoy it. You're looking forward to seeing everyone again soon." Instead, my inner voice told me that this chapter was over.

However, the sabotaging inner voice, which is fed by my beliefs, kept telling me the opposite. It said, "Don't be so stupid! You were successful in your job. You've earned good money and will probably continue to do so. That's what you can do, what you've always done. Starting something new again at fifty—are you crazy? You can't leave everyone in the lurch, that's not what you do! If you're in for a penny, you're in for a pound. You've decided to take on the responsibility and now you have to see it through. Who says that work always has to be fun?", and so on. I could now see this inner critic for what it was: harsh and unhelpful to me.

I felt that my benevolent inner voice knew me very, very well, better than anyone else in the world, and that it knew exactly what was best for me. So, after almost five months off, I met with my long-time friend and business partner in a café and told him that I would no longer be renewing my management board contract, which was due to expire shortly anyway. This contract had been set for renewal every three years, and each time previously, it had been extended without question. It was a very tough decision, one of the most difficult of my life, but to this day, I have never doubted for a second that it was the right move.

Unfortunately, my business partner didn't take that decision well and our friendship has been *on ice* ever since. Although his initial reaction to my breakdown had been very caring, the relationship had already cooled off during my months off. I increasingly felt that he did not understand me. I realized it was best to have some distance from him as well, since, because of our job, he was likely the person I had spent the most time with over the last twenty-two years. Unfortunately, during my time off, our conversations often revolved around money and formalities more than I would have liked, and certainly more than was beneficial for me. The mutual trust that had sustained us for so long was crumbling more and more, and obviously on both sides.

Recognizing the Power of Your Inner Voice

After I made the decision to leave the company and let everyone know, I often found myself thinking about that brilliant inner voice of mine that practically hit me over the head to stop me from heading straight into disaster. And then, with compassionate, patient gentleness, it showed me the right path and gave me a lot of strength and courage along the way.

During my research, I found that there are many synonyms for the benevolent inner voice, but they don't always mean exactly the same thing. Terms such as intuition, gut feeling, inner wisdom, or voice of the heart are often used to describe the phenomenon. However, while all of these terms point to a deeper, often unconscious form of guidance, they differ in their nuance and meaning.

Intuition, for example, is often understood as a sudden insight that arises without conscious thought—a knowing that seems to come out of nowhere. Gut feeling, on the other hand, refers more to a physically tangible reaction that is often inextricably linked to our emotional experiences. The inner wisdom indicates a source of deep, experienced knowledge that has been formed over years, while the heart voice is often associated with emotions, compassion, and moral sense.

Each of these synonyms has its own coloring and emphasis, and they all point to different aspects of how we are guided and directed internally. They illustrate that the inner voice can appear in many forms and that its manifestations are as diverse as the experiences and perspectives that people carry within them. Although they differ in their manifestation, all these terms have one thing in common: they invite us to listen to a deeper level of our consciousness and to be guided by an inner source that lies beyond logic and external influences.

I found out for myself that my inner voice is probably an interplay of rational thinking, emotional processing, and body perceptions.

41

Also, I learned that this phenomenon, which may seem esoteric or supernatural to some people, can be explained in biological terms. Scientists usually explain the inner voice as a complex interplay of different brain regions and biological mechanisms that together produce what we perceive as a benevolent inner voice. In the following, I will try to summarize what I consider to be the most important aspects in a way that is understandable for non-scientists (like myself).

How Our Brain Supports the Inner Voice

From a neurological perspective—i.e., looking at how our brain works—the benevolent inner voice is often associated with the limbic system, which plays a central role in processing emotions. The limbic system, which includes the amygdala, hippocampus, and other structures, is responsible for generating and storing emotional responses. You could think of the limbic system as the core of the brain, located deep inside and surrounded by the higher, rational structures of the cortex. When we have positive, supportive thoughts or sensations, the limbic system is active and helps us to feel a sense of security and well-being.

The prefrontal cortex, which lies directly behind the forehead, is the part of the brain responsible for higher cognitive functions such as planning, decision-making, and self-reflection. It plays a key role in regulating emotions and evaluating situations. When the benevolent inner voice speaks, the prefrontal cortex is involved by supporting positive beliefs and rational thoughts that contribute to healthy self-perception and emotional stability.

In order for our brain to function optimally and for our inner voice to speak to us, it needs suitable impulses. These impulses are mediated by hormones and neurotransmitters such as oxytocin. Oxytocin is produced in the hypothalamus, a kind of tiny control center deep in the brain, roughly in the middle of the head, and only about the size of a pea. Oxytocin is transported from there to the pituitary gland, which is located directly under the hypothalamus. The pituitary gland then releases oxytocin into the bloodstream. Oxytocin is also known as the *cuddle hormone* because it plays an important role in social bonding and feelings of trust and security. When people listen to their benevolent inner voice, oxytocin is released, which increases feelings of safety and emotional support. This hormone promotes positive social interactions and a sense of belonging, making the inner voice a strengthening, calming influence.

By releasing and spreading hormones through the bloodstream in the body, the brain can also trigger bodily reactions and sensations. Body perceptions play an important role in our perception of our inner voice, because it manifests physically.

The Role of the Body: Somatic Markers and Gut Feelings

This is how Portuguese neuroscientist Antonio Damasio, a professor at the University of Southern California (USC), developed the somatic marker hypothesis. Put simply, somatic markers are physical reactions or sensations (e.g., a queasy feeling in the stomach, sweating, accelerated heartbeat) that are associated with emotional experiences. These markers arise through the activation of the autonomic nervous system and are a kind of *alarm sign* or *feeling* that signals to the brain whether a certain action is good or bad for us. The somatic reactions develop from previous experiences that were emotionally significant. If we have experienced a certain action with negative consequences in the past, this experience is stored in our brain together with a physical reaction. Then later on if we are in a similar situation, this physical reaction (*somatic marker*) is activated again and serves as a warning signal. The hypothesis is that somatic markers help the brain to decide faster and more efficiently by letting us intuitively feel which options are good or bad for us even before we rationally analyze them. These markers influence our emotional judgment and can protect us from bad decisions by evoking unpleasant physical sensations that prevent us from taking dangerous or unfavorable actions. This means that we rely not only on logical reasoning, but also on the emotional and physical signals that are anchored in our brain. The somatic marker hypothesis shows that body awareness is essential for us if we wish to hear our benevolent inner voice, as it intuitively guides us through our bodily signals and helps us to make decisions that are in line with our deeply rooted emotional experiences and needs.

Many people experience the benevolent inner voice as a gut feeling or a feeling that comes from deep in the center of the body. This is due to the enteric nervous system (ENS), also known as the *second brain*. The ENS is a network of nerve cells in the gastrointestinal tract that functions independently of the central nervous system. It is closely connected to the vagus nerve. The vagus nerve is unique because it has the most extensive and diverse connections of all the cranial nerves. It runs from the brain through the neck and chest into the abdomen and supplies a variety of organs, including the heart, lungs, and digestive tract. It is an important part of the parasympathetic nervous system and plays a crucial role in the regulation of rest, digestion, and emotional well-being. The ENS processes emotional reactions and sends signals to the brain, and which can be perceived as intuitive insights or calming impulses. This gut feeling is often an expression of the benevolent inner voice, which fulfills a calming and supportive function at the level of the body and mind.

Why Evolution Shaped Your Inner Guide

Why does the human body have all these cool and (at least for me) fascinating features to help us do the right thing in life? Modern humans (*Homo sapiens*) in their current anatomical form have existed for about 200,000 to 300,000 years, depending on the definition. So, for at least 200,000 years, humans have had the appearance and physical characteristics we have today—including a larger cranial capacity to accommodate a larger brain and a highly developed capacity for language and abstract thought. In terms of evolutionary biology, we inherited a lot from our ancestors during this time (and even before, as the predecessors of *Homo sapiens* date back several million years), which was of fundamental importance for the survival of our species at the time. In this context, the benevolent inner voice can also be seen as a kind of survival mechanism that helps humans to make safe and useful decisions. Intuition and positive inner guidance may have evolved to help people avoid danger and take advantage of favorable opportunities. This inner voice may have originally served to stabilize people in social groups and help them to survive in difficult situations by drawing on feelings of safety and social support. We can, therefore, trust in a kind of *primal voice* that has evolved and been perfected over hundreds of thousands of years. However, it seems that, until today, we have been regressing for several decades and have often forgotten how to use this wonderful feature within us effectively.

In modern psychiatry and psychology, the concept of the benevolent inner voice is often associated with self-compassion. Kristin Neff, Professor of Educational Psychology at the

University of Texas at Austin and a leading researcher in the field of self-compassion, emphasizes that self-compassion involves being kind and understanding with oneself, especially during difficult times. This attitude fosters a positive, supportive inner voice that helps us to cope with stress and develop emotional resilience. Self-compassion activates networks in the brain that are associated with positive emotions and self-care, and helps to reduce negative emotional states such as anxiety and self-criticism. Also, Tara Brach emphasizes the great importance of bringing compassion to oneself in books such as *Radical Acceptance*. She is an American psychologist, author, and Insight Meditation teacher. Tara Brach emphasizes that self-compassion involves recognizing our own suffering with kindness and understanding, rather than judgment or criticism. She explains that by embracing self-compassion, we can free ourselves from the cycle of self-blame and open up to healing and emotional resilience. She is a guiding teacher and founder of the Insight Meditation Community of Washington, D.C. Brach holds a Ph.D. in Clinical Psychology and has completed extensive training in Buddhist meditation.

At the beginning of my crisis and coping with it, I could do little with the concept of self-compassion. I think I was waiting and thirsting to receive compassion from others during this phase. However, as this seems to be a rare commodity in this day and age, I had to learn (and feel this is a great gift) that the most reliable, effective, and (with practice) easiest way to get compassion is from myself.

Personally, it reassured and empowered me to realize that the inner voice is not some kind of esoteric hocus-pocus. No, the inner voice really does exist, even from a scientific point of view. In my opinion, it can be explained very conclusively and plausibly. At the same time, dealing with the scientifically researched principles also provided me with comprehensible explanations as to what was *wrong* with me and why I had lost contact with my inner voice.

Exercise 3

Connect with Your Inner Voice Through Body Awareness

Goal of the exercise

This exercise is designed to strengthen your connection with your benevolent inner voice through mindful body awareness. By practicing regularly, you will learn to tune into your inner voice by consciously focusing on your physical sensations. Over time, this will help you harness its positive influence more effectively in your daily life, allowing you to use its guidance and power with increasing ease and confidence.

Instructions

Step 1.

Choose a place where you will be undisturbed. Sit down comfortably and close your eyes.

Step 2.

Breathe in and out deeply, and close your eyes. Start with a few deep breaths. Breathe in slowly through your nose and out through your mouth. Concentrate only on your breath.

Step 3.

Scan your body: wander through your body from toe to head with your attention. Gradually feel each region of your body—your toes, feet, legs, genital area, stomach, chest, arms, shoulders, back, neck, and your head. Notice what sensations are present there—warmth, coolness, tension, relaxation, pain. Take a few minutes to do this, you are in no hurry. Don't judge, just notice. There is nothing to achieve, just perceive what is.

Step 4.

Focus on your core: direct your attention to your abdomen, the center of your core. Feel how your belly rises and falls with each breath. Pay attention to whether you can perceive a certain feeling here—be it a slight tingling sensation, a warmth or simply a feeling of calm.

Step 5.

Ask your inner voice a question. In this state of relaxation, ask your inner voice a question that is currently on your mind—perhaps a decision you need to make or an issue that is close to your heart. Listen for the answer, which may come in the form of a feeling or thought. Pay attention to how your body reacts to it. Let the thought or feeling go. Then ask the question again and repeat the process. Give the feeling space in the center of your body. Don't give the answer through active rational thinking (for me, this is the hardest part).

Step 6.

Write down your impressions. After a few minutes, open your eyes and write down what you have noticed. Perhaps it was a feeling of clarity, a gentle impulse, or a certain thought that emerged in your consciousness. Also make a note of what felt *right* and what felt *wrong* during this experience, without trying to explain or justify it rationally. It's all about your feelings.

Remark

If you didn't feel anything during the exercise, that is also a realization and is completely fine. You still have a few chapters ahead of you in this book to get closer to your inner voice. Depending on how much you have muted your inner voice, it will take some training to bring it out again.

Chapter VI

The Price of Ignoring Your Inner Voice

In the previous chapter, I went into more detail about the fact that the inner voice can actually be explained scientifically and in terms of evolutionary biology. So, it's not imaginary, it really exists! And now you might say: "Yes, okay. But is it relevant for me at all? I no longer live in caves, there are no wild animals that I have to watch out for and when I'm hungry or thirsty, I go to the fridge or the supermarket. Apart from that, I live my life and can't really complain, except for the small or big everyday problems that we all have somehow. So why should I work on listening to my inner voice?"

The Risks You Face

I have three answers to this:

1. Not listening to your inner voice can lead to really bad decisions in life. These can bring you concrete disadvantages in your family life, your social relationships, your job, or your finances.

2. Not listening to your inner voice can make you ill. I am living proof of this, because it made me ill; I couldn't work for a long time, and had to significantly reduce my social life.

3. Not listening to your inner voice can make you feel great regret at the end of your life when it's too late (and that's what I find most tragic). You'll say, "Oh boy. Why was I so blind? If only I had ..."

I don't want to discuss the first answer too much. You actually know about it already. Ask yourself how many times you have been annoyed with yourself because you made a bad decision (or didn't make a decision at all—that is usually also a decision, namely the decision not to decide). And afterwards you said to yourself or even out loud: "I'm an idiot! I knew it beforehand! I should have listened to my gut feeling/my intuition/my inner voice." These decisions can also be supposedly small things, such as "Do I speak up in class/in a seminar and say the answer?", "Should I go meet up with my old friends, or cancel because I've got way too much going on?", "Do I watch my Netflix series endlessly or do I go to bed earlier tonight?", "Do I cook together with my partner or do we order fast food because we're so tired?".

The Health Consequences of Neglecting Inner Guidance

The second aspect is more critical. I experienced this myself, but it took me a while to accept it. When I said to my business partner on that Monday morning: "I can't do this anymore!", I initially thought I would take a vacation, a time-out, a sabbatical. Go hiking for a few days first. I thought, I'm overworked, my battery is flat, I have motivation problems, the midlife crisis is getting to me and my divorce has taken too much energy. It wasn't until three weeks later that I went to my general practitioner, who has known me for many years. He immediately certified that I was unable to work and referred me directly to a specialist in neurology and psychiatry. The doctors agreed that I was suffering from burnout syndrome, specifically acute exhaustion with depressive symptoms, including full-blown sleep problems. I learned that burnout is not classified as a medical condition but is recognized by the WHO in its International Classification of Diseases (ICD-11) as an occupational phenomenon, specifically related to chronic stress in the workplace that has not been successfully managed. It is characterized by three primary dimensions:

1. Emotional exhaustion: Feeling drained and fatigued, both mentally and physically, with diminished energy levels.

2. Depersonalization (or cynicism): Developing negative, detached, or cynical attitudes towards one's job and colleagues, leading to a sense of detachment or distancing from work.

3. Reduced personal accomplishment: A sense of inefficacy or incompetence, where the individual feels they are not achieving success or growth in their role.

I had it all, and I personally believed that the term burnout perfectly captured my experience. I felt utterly burned out. The fire inside me had gone out, the candle's wick was barely warm, and the candle itself was nearly burned down.

Apart from the fact that I was actually always exhausted and tired and had less drive and joy than usual, I was doing quite well physically. Okay, my blood pressure was occasionally a little too high and I had chronic neck tension, but the fact that an illness can also have psychological causes and symptoms and not physical ones was new to me. I thought, that's only true for others, but not for me. I'm very resilient and have always managed this workload.

Burnout and the Body-Mind Connection

It's important to note that each individual's experience with burnout and emotional struggles is unique. While some people find relief through therapy, meditation, or reconnecting with their inner voice (I will come to that in more detail later), others may lean on different forms of support. Resilience—a person's ability to bounce back from difficult situations—plays a significant role in how one deals with stress and emotional exhaustion.

Resilience isn't just a personal trait but is also shaped by a mix of psychological, emotional, and social factors. Some people rely on strong social circles, such as friends or family, who offer emotional support during challenging times. Others find strength in their spiritual or religious beliefs, which can offer a sense of purpose and hope. Additionally, past experiences in overcoming hardships can build internal strength, making it easier to silence the bad inner voice in the face of new challenges.

For those who lack these support systems, the sense of isolation can make the feelings of alienation often associated with burnout even worse. Without psychological resilience or external social support, the journey through burnout can feel far more difficult, highlighting the importance of building and maintaining connections, whether they are familial, social, or spiritual.

Psychosomatic Illness: When Ignoring Your Voice Makes You Sick

It is true: constantly acting against their inner voice makes most people ill. This is supported by psychosomatic medicine and modern stress research.

Psychosomatics deals with the connection between psychological stress and physical symptoms. When a person persistently ignores their inner needs and beliefs or acts against their nature, this can lead to a chronic state of stress, dissatisfaction and inner tension. Chronic stress can significantly impact both physical and mental health by triggering a variety of symptoms. Research shows that elevated stress hormones, such as cortisol, are associated with a higher risk of developing hypertension and cardiovascular events like heart attacks and strokes. Additionally, prolonged stress weakens the immune system, making the body more vulnerable to illness. This connection between psychological stress and physical health has been thoroughly examined in studies that reveal how stress-related hormone imbalances can lead to heart disease, digestive issues, and other physical ailments.

On a psychological level, ignoring the inner voice can lead to depression, anxiety, and burnout. When people do not live their true needs and desires, they can develop a feeling of emptiness, alienation, or meaninglessness, which affects their mental health.

If what a person does every day is not in line with their inner values and beliefs, they realize this and inner conflicts arise, as their rational mind keeps trying to explain to them that everything is just as it should be—a bit like the famous angels and devils on the left and right shoulder who give us contradictory advice. This can lead to a state of chronic dissatisfaction and inner turmoil, which manifests itself in the form of psychological complaints. As explained in the previous chapter, the inner voice often acts as an early warning system, signaling when something in our lives is not in line with our true needs and values. If these signals are ignored because we allow ourselves to be guided by, for example, external expectations or social norms, this can lead to a state of chronic inner dissonance that has a negative impact on our body and mind.

Long-term disregard of the inner voice can therefore lead to both physical and psychological symptoms of illness, as the body tries to communicate the imbalance in other ways.

However, there are obviously many people who do not listen to their inner voice but are, as mentioned above, more resilient, and thus still manage to get through life in a reasonably healthy way. This is perhaps a bit like smoking: it is undeniably unhealthy and many people get sick sooner or later as a result. Yet there are also people who seem less affected by it, and of course you could be lucky enough to be one of them.

Regrets of the Dying: A Lesson in Listening

Even if you are among the physically resilience ones, I still have some bad news. It seems that at the end of our lives, in the face of death, which we become increasingly aware of due to a serious illness, for example, or simply in the face of progressive physical decline, we develop a greater clarity about our past life. It's a great thing when you hear an elderly person say something like: "I had a good life. I am very grateful for everything and would do everything exactly the same again." Of course, there is such a possibility and for me personally, it is my most important goal in life: to die without regrets. That was also the reason why I was so interested in reading the book *The Top 5 Regrets of the Dying* after I happened to read a review of it in a newspaper years ago. The author is Bronnie Ware, an Australian and former palliative care nurse. She has spent years accompanying people in the weeks and months before they die. She is obviously a wonderful and highly empathetic woman who spoke to many of these people about their lives and their regrets when looking back on life. I thought to myself quite pragmatically: Who can you get better life advice from than people who have already lived a whole life and are now drawing conclusions? The book moved me deeply; it made me think, fascinated me, and inspired me. Today I know that all of these *Top 5 Regrets of the Dying* can be traced back to whether or not people have followed their inner voice on the really important things in the course of their lives. This is absolutely amazing to me, because this shows me how important it really is to take this inner voice seriously, because it wants to help us to lead a life that we can look back on with gratitude and satisfaction at some point and thus depart this earthly life in peace. So, what were these top five regrets and what do they have to do with the inner voice? I list them below, and build a bridge to the inner voice for each one.

I wish I'd had the courage to live a life true to myself, not the life others expected of me.

A man worked his whole life as a lawyer because his father expected him to, even though he always wanted to be a musician. At the end of his life, he felt deep sadness that he never found the courage to pursue his true passion and live his own life.

This regret shows that many people have ignored their own inner voice and instead followed the expectations of others.

They did not live authentically according to their own values and wishes.

I wish I hadn't worked so hard.

A businessman planned to take a trip around the world with his wife after his retirement, but kept putting it off because he wanted to close the next big deal. Tragically, his wife suddenly fell seriously ill and died before they could realize their dream together. The man severely blamed himself until his death, as he realized that none of the deals meant anything for him retroactively.

Here, regret indicates that the inner voice often calls for balance and time for essentials such as shared experiences with loved ones, but many ignore these needs in favor of career and success on the outside.

I wish I'd had the courage to express my feelings.

A woman lived in a cold, distant marriage because she never dared to tell her husband how unhappy she was. On her deathbed, she regretted that she never found the courage to express her true feelings and stand up for her own happiness.

This remorse shows that people often suppress their true feelings and needs because they are afraid of rejection or conflict. However, the inner voice encourages authenticity and honesty.

I wish I had stayed in touch with my friends.

A woman lost contact with her closest friends over the years because she became too involved in caring for her sick mother and hardly had any time for herself or her social relationships. When she finally fell seriously ill herself, she deeply regretted that she had not invested more time in her friendships, which could have offered her so much comfort and support.

The desire for deep and meaningful relationships is often a quiet but persistent voice within us. This regret shows that people have neglected their social needs and connections.

I wish that I had let myself be happier.

A successful executive spent his life living up to constant societal expectations and putting more and more pressure on himself to be *successful*. As he lay dying, he realized that he had never given himself permission to just be and enjoy the simple pleasures of life, which ultimately denied him true contentment.

This regret reveals that many people ignore the inner voice that guides them towards joy and contentment in life. Instead, they remain trapped in old patterns and fears.

I was very moved by these stories, probably because I recognized myself in more than one of the regrets. None of these five regrets is particularly spectacular; in fact, they are very *basic*. We all know that! Yet we still neglect the described aspects of life too often, because we don't hear our inner voice or don't trust it enough.

Practical Advice: When to Trust Your Inner Voice and When to Pause

That said, a word of caution: I don't recommend following your inner voice blindly or in every situation. There are times when external responsibilities or practical considerations must take precedence. For example, in moments of intense fear, uncertainty, or emotional turmoil, your inner voice might be clouded by anxiety rather than being true intuition. In these cases, it's essential to balance your inner guidance with careful reflection and, if needed, seek advice from trusted people or professionals. The key is to know when to listen and when to pause and evaluate.

Also, I don't mean that in future you should unconditionally say *yes* to everything nice and *no* to everything unpleasant. I am not preaching unconditional selfishness or hedonism at the expense of others. Rather, I am convinced that we too often chase after superficial entertainment and fleeting fun and adventure. Our inner voice tells us otherwise. Above all, it wants us a) to be safe and b) to be able to develop as much as possible in line with our own *secret life plan* so that we have no regrets at the end of our lives.

Exercise 4

Return to the Inner Truth

Goal of the exercise

This exercise aims to help you recognize moments when you've consciously suppressed your inner voice and to prevent this in the future. By reflecting on past decisions where your inner voice was ignored, you will develop the ability to align your choices more closely with it moving forward, making better decisions that are in harmony with your true self.

Instructions

Step 1. Identify a moment of doubt

Think of a situation in which you felt what was right for you, but chose to ignore this impulse. What made you ignore your inner voice?

Step 2. Visualize the consequences
Close your eyes and visualize the consequences of this decision. How did ignoring your inner voice affect your life? What feelings arose afterwards? Perhaps regret, frustration or a feeling of being lost?

Step 3. Consciously choose differently
Now imagine you could relive this situation. How would you act differently this time? What would change if you listened to your inner voice?

Step 4. Write a promise to yourself
Write down a promise to yourself in your notebook that you will listen to your inner voice more consciously in the future. This act of writing can help you to consolidate this promise and remember it in future situations.

Step 5. Reflection
At the end of the week or even at the end of the month, sit down again and reflect on how often you have listened to your inner voice and how it has influenced your life. Make a note of your findings to further strengthen your trust in your inner voice.

Chapter VII

The Hidden Forces Behind
Ignoring Your Inner Voice

I have just shown you where it can lead if we ignore our inner voice. The interesting question is: why do we do it anyway if it can make us ill or miserable?

Again, I have three answers for you.

1. The Weight of Responsibility

We play different roles in our lives and wear several hats. The further we step into adulthood, the truer this usually becomes. If we were lucky enough to meet the right person, we live in a love relationship. Successful and harmonious relationships also thrive on compromise and mutual consideration. We are (co-)responsible for the well-being of our partner (even if it can also be argued that everyone is responsible for

71

their own happiness). We have a job and are responsible for doing it well so that we earn money. We might also carry the responsibility of managing employees. If we have children, that is of course a huge responsibility, because the smaller children are, the more they depend on us parents; indeed, their survival depends on us. If we have bought an apartment or a house, we probably have to pay off a loan. We may still be involved in a community organization, whether it's volunteering at a school, serving in a local charity, or supporting social initiatives. At some point, our own parents will get older and need our help. This list could go on and on for some of us.

That's a good thing, because that's the only way societies can work. We need people who take responsibility, stand by their word, and stand up for others and help them. I love and admire people who shout *here* when it comes to taking responsibility. There are many examples of great people who are able to carry an extremely heavy load. Yet this only works up to a certain point. In other words, it only works as long as this burden doesn't become too heavy and doesn't permanently *compromise* their own wishes and needs.

Research shows that societal expectations often lead people to prioritize external duties, which can create internal conflicts when their personal desires are consistently ignored. Everyone has their own limits and we are not all the same (thank God). It is therefore important not to forget one thing despite all responsibility towards others: responsibility towards yourself!

2. The Comfort Trap

In general, people tend to seek being comfortable. This also has a sound basis in psychology and behavioral research. People often remain in environments, routines, or behaviors that are familiar and comfortable to them. Within this comfort zone, people feel safe and less stressed as they do not have to deal with any major challenges or changes.

People also tend to repeat behaviors that are rewarding or avoid negative consequences. Avoiding risks and sticking to familiar, safe behaviors is therefore a natural human tendency. This increases as we get older. One reason for this is the neuroplasticity of the brain. Research indicates that neuroplasticity, the brain's ability to adapt and reorganize itself, decreases as we age. While younger brains are more flexible and capable of rapid learning and adaptation, studies show that adults experience significantly less neural plasticity as they age, compared to younger adults. This reduced flexibility can make it harder to learn new skills or adapt to changes. So, as people get older, they tend to increasingly look for psychological security, i.e., stable, predictable living conditions. This security is often found in the comfort zone, where life holds fewer surprises and challenges. However, it's important to note that although neuroplasticity declines, it doesn't stop entirely, and activities like regular exercise, mental challenges, and social engagement can help maintain brain health into older age.

Looking back, I realize that it was the same for me: at a certain age, after I had achieved a lot in life that I had never dared to dream of as a young person, my *voice of reason* told me: "Objectively speaking, everything is good and has to stay exactly the same. That's what you've always wanted. Stop going crazy and putting it at risk!" By comfort, I don't mean laziness. On the contrary, some people are very hardworking and active in their comfort zone, and I was too, mainly to maintain this comfort zone and not have to push the boundaries or venture into unknown territory or jump into cold water.

3. The Paralyzing Power of Fear

The further we have come in life, the more we have built up and accumulated, both materially and in terms of relationships, then the more afraid we are of losing some of it again. We are also afraid of failure, and afraid of the unfamiliar (of moving well outside our comfort zone). Yet what is most important for most people in their lives is other people. Humans are extremely social creatures.

Even the biggest loners can't avoid having one or two social relationships. At least in the closest family circle, people in our society today are more or less bound to their blood relatives for their entire lives, even if it is only through the beliefs that have been ingrained in their subconscious since childhood. In other words, above all we are afraid of rejection from parents, siblings, life partners, friends, our own children, bosses, business partners, or even colleagues at work. The question: "What will that person think of me then? Will they no longer love me? Will they leave me?" inhibits most of us from following our inner voice.

Psychological research has demonstrated that fear of social rejection is actually one of the strongest inhibitors of behavior, often leading individuals to suppress their inner voice in favor of maintaining social acceptance.

These resistances that I have described here are strong opponents to the inner voice. I have experienced this myself. Looking back, I realized that my inner voice had not been completely silenced. I even *lent it my voice* in brief, light moments. In private conversations with close friends outside my immediate business circle, I had already voiced, more than once, a vague wish to "just take a longer break." I had also told my business partner in an all-day offsite meeting more than six months before my *breakdown* that "I don't want to and I can't carry on like this for much longer". But the next day I was back to everyday life and responsibility, as comfort and fear took over again. Things continued more or less as before, because they had to. The supposedly sensible voice quickly regained the upper hand and said: "Now don't spook the horses and be sensible." And I was reasonable for as long as I could. Until I couldn't be anymore.

Exercise 5

The Inner Resistance—
Recognize and Overcome It

Goal of the exercise

This exercise helps you to identify the main reasons why you ignore your inner voice and to find ways to overcome this resistance.

Instructions

Step 1. Identify the resistance

Think about a circumstance in your life that makes you feel like you are ignoring your inner voice. Write down what exactly is preventing you from following it—is it a sense of responsibility, comfort, fear, or something else?

Step 2. Reflect on the consequences

Tink about how these resistances affect your life. What are the likely short-term and long-term effects of not listening to your inner voice? Write these thoughts down.

Step 3. Create a counter-strategy

For each identified resistance, think of a possible strategy to overcome it. For example, how can you take more responsibility for your own needs without neglecting your obligations to others? How can you leave your comfort zone step by step?

Step 4. Take one small, courageous action

Choose one small action you can implement in the next few days to be more mindful of your inner voice, even if it's just a small step at first. Write down how it made you feel and what you learned from it.

Chapter VIII

Reconnecting with Your Inner Voice: Techniques to Find Your Center

So, there are many reasons for not paying attention to our inner voice or not following what it wants to tell us. In addition to the inner resistance that I outlined in the previous chapter, it is often the external circumstances of our hectic lives that prevent us from seeing (or hearing) what is important. Everything is becoming faster, more hectic, and more fleeting.

Above all, the internet and the triumph of smartphones and social media platforms have changed our lives dramatically. Many of us are always *on*, always available and usually not fully present in the real world, but with at least half of our attention elsewhere.

While I advocate for reducing the use of social media, especially as a way to reconnect with your inner voice, it's important to acknowledge that social media itself isn't inherently bad. When used mindfully and with purpose, social media can actually be a powerful tool for promoting businesses, building meaningful connections, and gaining new knowledge. It offers the opportunity to learn, grow, and stay informed in ways that were never possible before.

However, the key is moderation and intentional use. The problem arises when social media use becomes mindless and habitual, pulling us away from being present and engaging deeply with our own thoughts or the people around us. Rather than cutting it out completely, I suggest using social media consciously—set specific times for it, use it for its productive aspects, and be aware of how it affects your emotions and mindset. By doing this, social media can become a tool that enhances your life rather than a distraction from it.

What's more, we generally spend a lot of time thinking about the future, a little about the past, and yet we get so little of the present—but that's where we live.

Cultivating Mindfulness in Everyday Life

I came across the following short anecdote, or something similar, in a mindfulness course (MBSR = mindfulness-based stress reduction; more on this below). It describes the principle of mindfulness and the difference between being mindful and doing it automatically.

A student asks a Zen master: "Master, what is the secret of your happy and fulfilled life?" The master replies: "It's actually quite simple: when I work, I work. When I eat, I eat. When I walk, I walk. And when I sleep, I sleep." The student is confused and says: "But Master, don't all people do that? What's so special about it?" The master replies: "No, most people do it a little differently: when they work, they think about eating. When they eat, they think about walking. When they walk, they think about sleeping. And when they sleep, they wake up and think about working. So, they are never really in the moment."

We have to learn to be with ourselves again. I have explained to you that the inner voice is probably an interplay of rational thinking, emotional feelings, and body perceptions. We can only hear the inner voice when there is *quietness* both outside and inside us.

81

The following techniques and habits have helped many people, including myself, to be more in touch with themselves, to find their own *center* again and ultimately to be in contact with their own feelings and needs. In short: listening to your inner voice and being in dialogue with yourself.

Meditation and Mindfulness

These practices are excellent for calming the mind and connecting with your inner voice. They help you to reduce the inner chatter and create space for deeper insights.

As I mentioned before, I learned meditation and mindfulness in an MBSR (mindfulness-based stress reduction) course developed by Jon Kabat-Zinn, an American professor emeritus of medicine from New York. The MBSR course is an eight-week program that aims to reduce stress through mindfulness. At the heart of the MBSR course is the development of mindfulness, which means perceiving the present moment consciously and without judgment. Participants learn to focus their attention on the breath, body sensations, thoughts, and emotions. Formal exercises include body scan, mindfulness meditation, and gentle yoga exercises. In addition to the formal exercises, the practice of informal mindfulness is also taught, in which everyday activities such as eating, walking, or even washing the dishes are carried out with full attention. The MBSR course aims to strengthen the abilities of self-awareness and self-regulation, to better manage stress and to improve overall mental and physical well-being.

I found the MBSR course to be a very powerful tool for paying less attention to inner and outer noise. It helped me become kinder and more benevolent towards myself, ultimately allowing me to reconnect with myself and my inner voice.

Hiking, Jogging, Cycling

Physical activity in nature can have a very calming and grounding effect. These activities not only promote physical health, but also offer time and space for reflection and inner contemplation. This applies to endurance activities where the heart rate does not get too high. Depending on your fitness level, it should not exceed 120-140 beats per minute in order to maintain this intensity over a longer period of time and get into a flow. I see many people who run with headphones and either listen to music or use their time efficiently and listen to podcasts. My personal experience is that listening to the sounds of nature and being in the here and now, i.e., running without headphones, promotes mindfulness. In addition to the tangible physical experience of running—the contact of my feet with the ground, the sweat, and the gradually tiring muscles—my thoughts become increasingly focused during endurance sports in nature. I rarely have such clear thoughts and often find the answers to questions that have been on my mind for a while with ease, almost effortlessly.

Of course, swimming is also an endurance sport. I have left it out here for two reasons. Firstly, it is usually done in a stuffy, chlorinated swimming pool and you don't experience nature. Secondly, I don't like swimming and I'm not particularly good at it. Yet I know that there are people who, while swimming endless laps in their fashionable swim cap and goggles, enter into a state similar to meditation. This seems like a good moment to add a suggestion: give swimming a try.

Sauna and Massages

As well as its scientifically proven beneficial health effects, heat can help to release physical and mental tension, which in turn makes it easier to access your inner voice. I love going to the sauna on colder or rainy days. I find the extreme warmth and the sweat on my skin, and also the subsequent cold of the shower or ice bath, and the overall peace and quiet in the sauna, have many beneficial effects. They help me calm down, sort out my thoughts, connect with my body, and consciously perceive it. On an emotional level, I get a feeling of self-care, self-compassion, and security. Similarly, massages can have a positive effect by stimulating the muscles, which generates warmth and promotes relaxation. In addition, the act of touch during a massage has been shown to positively influence the release of hormones such as oxytocin, contributing to an overall sense of well-being. It also can give you inspiration. A friend of mine even called me after he got a massage to suggest a title for this book, having glanced at the manuscript right before the massage.

Open Discussions

Exchanging ideas with others, especially people with different life circumstances, can open up new perspectives and promote self-reflection. Ask each other uncomfortable questions such as "What would you do if you were not subject to external constraints? What change would you make if you could or if you didn't have to reckon with bad consequences? If you did, what would be the worst thing that could happen?" Don't take the easy way out by answering that you just want to hang out on the beach or on the imaginary yacht and sip cocktails, because in the vast majority of cases, that's not what we really want and what a fulfilled life means to us. Don't worry, you only have to talk about it at first and not turn it into reality straight away. But your thoughts are free and it can be very helpful to talk about them in order to make your inner voice heard in the truest sense of the word.

Freewriting

Freewriting is a writing exercise in which you write continuously for a certain period of time (by hand and not on a computer or smartphone) without putting down the pen and without thinking too much about the content. The focus is on allowing the flow of thoughts without censoring yourself or interrupting the writing process. The aim is to activate the subconscious and switch off the *inner censor* so that ideas and solutions that might normally be suppressed come to the surface.

Specifically, it involves formulating a problem ("The problem is ...") and then writing whatever comes to mind without interruption. Even if it seems nonsensical at first, this process can help to release blockages and find new perspectives or solutions to the problem. The technique uses the flow of thoughts and can help to discover unusual connections or intuitive insights that might not have occurred to you through conscious thought. The inner voice should therefore make its way onto the paper via the hand and pen.

Psychotherapy

In my opinion, a psychotherapist should not only be consulted in exceptional psychological situations or acute states of depression. In my experience, psychotherapy can also be very helpful in reconnecting with your inner voice. It can help people to resolve inner conflicts, identify emotional blockages, and understand themselves better. This allows them to regain access to their inner voice, i.e., their deep convictions, values, and feelings.

Psychotherapy promotes self-reflection and mindfulness, two essential components for recognizing the inner voice. Therapeutic conversations help to bring to light unconscious patterns and beliefs that often override or block the connection to one's inner voice.

As we have already seen, many people have learned to ignore their inner voice over the course of their lives, often due to learned behavioral patterns. In therapy, these blockages can be worked on, which makes it possible to listen better to one's own needs and beliefs again.

Despite the proven benefits of psychotherapy, there is unfortunately still a stigma around seeking psychotherapeutic help in many cultures and societies. People fear being seen as *weak* or *crazy* if they start therapy, which often leads to feelings of shame. The acceptance of psychotherapy varies greatly between different countries and cultures. In many Western countries such as the USA, Canada, and Northern Europe, especially in countries such as Sweden and the Netherlands, psychotherapy is increasingly accepted and even seen as part of general health care. In countries with a stronger cultural emphasis on strength and independence, such as some Asian and South American cultures, the stigma can be greater and the uptake of therapy remains comparatively low. In many Asian countries, such as Japan and China, there are cultural barriers to seeking psychotherapy. The pressure not to show *weakness* and the expectation to solve problems within the family contribute to a higher degree of stigmatization. In South America, there are differences between countries. In Brazil, for example, the acceptance of psychotherapy is relatively high, while in other countries in the region the stigma is still very pronounced. In Southern European countries, such as Italy and Spain, psychotherapy is also used, but there are still reservations and stigmatization, especially in more rural areas. In urban areas, however, acceptance is greater.

For me personally, two effects of psychotherapy in particular were very effective, as well as astonishing. Firstly, I felt empathy from a neutral person with whom I had no social relationship. This may also have been due to the individual nature of the therapist. It was very good for me because I felt heard, taken seriously, and no longer so alone with my problem, which the therapist also recognized and respected as such. On the other hand, I was asked some very good questions—seemingly simple, yet obviously straightforward questions for an outsider, such as "Are you sure that you and *so-and-so* are still such good friends? Is this how a good friend behaves? Is this what you need from them as a friend right now?". That opened my eyes, because the answer gradually made its way into me and became clearer and clearer: "Well, no, not really."

Dopamine Diet

Most of us live in a state of excessive dopamine release these days. Dr. Anna Lembke's *Dopamine Nation* really reshaped my understanding of this topic.

Dr. Lembke is an American psychiatrist, and professor of psychiatry and behavioral sciences at Stanford University School of Medicine. She is also head of the Department of Addiction Medicine at Stanford and specializes in addiction research.

I learned from her that dopamine is a neurotransmitter that plays a central role in our brain's reward system. It is responsible for creating the feeling of pleasure and reward and motivates us to repeat actions that give us this pleasure.

Dopamine is released when we do something that our brain perceives as positive and rewarding, such as eating, having sex, or achieving a goal.

Nowadays, there are numerous sources that provide us with quick dopamine kicks. The list is long and getting longer:

- Social media: every *like*, notification, or message can trigger a little dopamine rush, causing us to constantly check our smartphone.

- Junk food: highly processed foods that are high in sugar, salt and fat activate the reward system and encourage excessive consumption.

- Gambling: both real gambling and gambling in the form of video games or mobile games can cause a strong release of dopamine.

- Alcohol and drugs: substances such as alcohol, nicotine, and other drugs can also lead to a strong release of dopamine, resulting in addiction. In the long run, these substances also ruin the mechanism of action of your neurotransmitters, which are responsible for relaxation and joy, and deprive you of important vitamins and minerals.

- (Online) shopping: buying new things, especially in the form of impulse purchases, can cause a quick but short-term high.
- Streaming services: binge-watching series or movies provides continuous, quick rewards that release dopamine.

Now, why is this harmful? Dr. Lembke describes that too much dopamine stimulation causes the brain to become imbalanced. When the initial high wears off, dopamine levels drop, which can lead to a state of dopamine deficiency. This can lead to depression, anxiety, and loss of motivation as the brain responds to this overstimulation by reducing its sensitivity to dopamine. Constant dopamine kicks from external sources can lead to the development of addictions, as the brain needs more of what previously made it happy to achieve the same effect. Long-term overstimulation of the dopamine system can lead to normal activities that once brought pleasure no longer being perceived as satisfying. This leads to a downward spiral in which stronger and stronger stimuli are needed to experience the same feeling of pleasure.

The constant search for external rewards overrides the signals of the inner voice. Instead of listening to inner needs and genuine feelings, short-term, superficial rewards are favored. Dopamine-stimulated activities such as social media, excessive shopping, or gambling constantly distract us, which impairs our ability to look inward and listen to what we really want or need. When dopamine becomes the dominant driving force, we lose access to deeper emotions and values. This can distract us from making authentic decisions that are in line with our inner voice.

I got my dopamine kicks and distraction from myself mainly from alcohol and the regular (and often unnecessary) use of my smartphone; two *bad habits* that are a permanent and recognized part of most societies in this world. At some point, I imposed rules on myself when I found out that it is simply very difficult to do less of it or not do it at all. I've deleted a few apps from my smartphone and regularly do a *Digital Detox Sunday*, where I switch off all mobile data on my smartphone for a day. This gives me much more peace and quiet and less internal distraction. As far as alcohol is concerned, I'm currently on a self-imposed one-year abstinence as I write this book. This will be my longest alcohol-free period in roughly thirty-five years. For many years now, I have always taken one *sober* month, or sometimes six weeks, every year. The longest period so far has been 100 days without alcohol. I have had the simple but clear experience that I always feel better without alcohol than with it. I sleep better, wake up in the morning with more energy, have a clearer head, am more self-confident, more decisive, eat more consciously, and exercise more regularly. Of course, during this period of abstinence, I often get strange looks in my social environment. Other people around me who drink alcohol (or rather, too much alcohol) obviously feel worse when they are confronted with the fact that you could drink little or even nothing at all and that some people even do this. If you want to get away from socially accepted everyday drugs such as nicotine or alcohol, I recommend the books by Allen Carr (*The Easy Way To ...*). They have helped me (I used to smoke too) because they clear up the self-deception (he calls it brainwashing) in our heads and make quitting amazingly easy without missing it or regretting it.

Books and Podcasts

Engaging with inspiring content can raise your awareness and encourage your inner voice to speak out. This can be the content in novels as well as non-fiction books that make you engage with yourself. I myself learned a key lesson from the book *The Alchemist* by the Brazilian author Paulo Coelho as a young adult. Since then, I have read it every now and then or listened to it as an audio book. The book tells the story of the young shepherd Santiago from Andalusia, a region in the south of Spain. He dreams of a treasure hidden in Egypt at the foot of the pyramids. On his journey, he experiences many challenges and learns deep life lessons about love, courage, loss, and the pursuit of his dreams. In the end, however, it turns out that the treasure Santiago was looking for is in his homeland, exactly where his journey began. He had to make the whole journey to come to this realization— not because the treasure itself was important, but because the journey helped him grow, learn, and find his true purpose.

There are many other books that like *The Alchemist* have inspired me to reflect and *feel* about life and about myself.

After the last chapter of this book, I have included a short list with some recommendations.

Self-compassion

The principle of self-compassion was developed by Kristin Neff, the US psychologist and researcher from Texas that I mentioned earlier. It refers to treating yourself with the same kindness, care, and understanding as you would a friend or loved one, especially in difficult moments. It is a powerful way to promote emotional health and reduce stress, self-criticism, and negative emotions.

The principle of self-compassion can help you to better hear and follow your own inner voice. The key elements are:

1. Reduced self-criticism, more room for intuition

People who criticize themselves strongly often find it difficult to listen to their inner voice, as the negative self-assessment drowns out the quiet signals of intuition. Self-compassion helps to soften this inner criticism and thus opens up space for the benevolent inner voice that wants to guide us in a positive direction.

2. Mindfulness as a prerequisite for accessing the inner voice

Mindfulness is a central component of self-compassion. I have already explained that it is about being fully in the present moment without judgment. This presence and awareness are necessary in order to perceive the quiet impulses of the inner voice. Without mindfulness, you can easily become distracted and lose touch with your own deeper needs.

3. Courage to go your own way

Self-compassion gives you permission to make mistakes and learn from them without judging yourself. This reduces the fear of failure, making it easier to listen to your inner voice and make courageous decisions, even if they seem unconventional or risky.

4. Common humanity instead of isolation

When we recognize that our struggles and doubts are part of the human experience, it becomes easier to trust our inner voice. Self-compassion helps us to feel connected to other people and not feel alone in our challenges. This connection can strengthen our confidence to follow our own path.

Self-perception and Behavior

Even if you don't *hear* or feel your inner voice, observe your behavior and your body reactions. It is very important to cultivate this self-awareness. Ask: Does something literally make my stomach ache, do I actually feel the weight on my shoulders (as tension?), do I say one thing and do another? Then focus your observation on your actions in a completely non-judgmental way. For example, do you find it easy to go out with a certain friend and feel better afterwards? Yet with another friend, do you just keep looking for excuses to not meet up? Probably your inner voice, which influences your behavior, is trying to tell you something about these relationships. "Actions speak louder than words", a wise and dear friend once said to me.

This theory is similar to what is often referred to in psychology as the body-mind connection or somatic self-awareness. This theory states that the body often sends signals about our emotional states before we consciously recognize them. There are various scientific concepts that support this theory, such as the concept of embodied cognition in cognitive science, which states that our thoughts and emotions are strongly influenced by the body. This means that your behavior and body reactions are often an expression of your inner states, even if you are not immediately aware of them.

According to Antonio Damasio's somatic marker hypothesis, physical sensations (somatic markers) are closely linked to emotional experiences and help us to make decisions. If you feel physical reactions such as abdominal pain or tension in your shoulders, these markers may indicate that something in your environment or your relationships is not in line with your true needs. Your behavior and physical responses act as unconscious signals from your inner voice.

Mindfulness research shows that conscious awareness of physical sensations (such as tension or abdominal pain) can help us to recognize emotional and mental states. If you often feel tense around a certain friend or find yourself making excuses to avoid meeting them altogether, it may be a sign that your inner voice is signaling that this relationship is out of balance.

Cognitive dissonance describes the inner conflict that arises when our behavior does not match our beliefs or feelings. When you say one thing but do another (e.g., meeting a friend even though it doesn't feel right), this creates inner tension. Your body may react through physical symptoms as your inner voice tries to signal the inconsistency between your behavior and your true feelings.

Breathing Exercises

Breathing exercises are a powerful method of calming the mind and deepening access to the inner voice. They can also be referred to as light meditation or a preliminary stage to meditation. Breathing exercises help to activate the parasympathetic nervous system, which leads to relaxation and stress reduction. One simple exercise is to focus on your breathing by inhaling and exhaling deeply and evenly.

An example is the 4-4-4-4 breathing technique: Breathe in for four seconds, hold your breath for four seconds, breathe out for four seconds, and hold your breath again for four seconds. Repeat this cycle for a few minutes.

This exercise not only calms the mind, but also sharpens attention to the present moment. When the mind is calm, it becomes easier to perceive the inner voice, as it is often quiet and subtle.

It is helpful to regularly integrate breathing exercises into your daily routine—for example, in the morning after waking up or in the evening before going to bed—in order to continuously deepen this connection to your inner voice.

Rituals for Self-reflection

A self-reflection ritual in the morning or evening can be an important anchor in your daily routine, allowing you to pause and connect with your inner voice. These rituals help you to regularly focus on your own thoughts and feelings and thus develop a deeper self-awareness.

Morning ritual: After waking up, take five to ten minutes to sit quietly and organize your thoughts. Think about what is important to you for the coming day and what emotions you are feeling, and write them down in a diary. This can help you to use your inner voice as a guide for the day.

One of my closest and dearest friends has a morning ritual that I find very impressive. In one corner of his house, he has created a small, tranquil space with plants and wall art. Each morning, he lights incense, sits quietly for a few minutes, and recites his version of Buddhism's Five Truths to himself. It goes like this:

1. The death we cannot escape.
2. The aging we cannot escape.
3. The sickness we cannot escape.
4. All things we love and that belong to us in this life we have to give away one day.
5. All things we did, we do, and we will do, we carry with us.

He explained to me the benefit of this as follows: by reminding yourself daily that nothing lasts, you can start to appreciate simple things like health, freedom, food, and shelter more deeply. This ongoing awareness brings a sense of calm—and with it, greater contentment.

Evening ritual: Before going to bed, you can review the day. Think about which moments or encounters triggered special feelings in you. Were there situations in which you acted against your inner voice? Such rituals encourage regular reflection and can help you to be more aware of your inner voice in everyday life and to follow it.

Creative Forms of Expression

Creative activities such as painting, making music, writing, or dancing offer direct access to the inner voice, as they often express unconscious thoughts and feelings. Through creative forms of expression, we can address deeper emotional layers that are not so easily revealed in normal conversation or thinking.

Painting: Sit down with paints and a brush without thinking beforehand about what exactly you want to paint. Just let your hand paint what comes out of you intuitively. You will be surprised how often such creative activities make unconscious feelings or thoughts visible.

Make music: If you play an instrument or enjoy singing, you can put yourself in a state of free improvisation. By making music without a fixed goal, you open the channel to your inner voice, which can express itself in an intuitive way.

Creative activities help to bypass the inner critic and feel what is really important deep inside. Regularity is also crucial here in order to strengthen the connection to the inner voice through creative activities.

Exercise 6

Strengthening Self-awareness—Body and Behavior as a Mirror of the Inner Voice

Goal of the exercise

This exercise is designed to enhance your understanding of your inner voice by focusing on physical sensations and behaviors. It helps you recognize the signals your body and behavior give about your true needs and feelings. By developing awareness of these signals, you will learn to interpret them as valuable insights from your inner voice, even when it does not communicate directly through thoughts or words, thus fostering deeper self-awareness and connection.

Instructions

Step 1. Observe your body

Sit down in a quiet moment and consciously observe your body. Close your eyes and scan your body from toe to head.

Is there any tension, abdominal pain, or any other physical symptoms? Write down these sensations.

Step 2. Pay attention to your behavior patterns
Think about situations in which you regularly find excuses to avoid certain activities or appointments. What kind of relationships or commitments cause you to feel the need to make excuses? Make a note of the situations and the physical reactions you experience.

Step 3. Connect behavior and physical sensations
Think about whether there is a connection between your physical symptoms and your behavior. For example, do you feel tense after certain meetings or do you have stomach pains? What does your body tell you about these activities or relationships?

Step 4. Ask for the message
Write in free text, without putting down the pen, what these body sensations and behavior patterns want to tell you. Start with "My body is telling me that ..." and write what comes to mind.

Step 5. Reflect and act

Read through what you have written. Are there clear messages from your inner voice that you have ignored so far? What small steps could you take to respond to these signals? Write down at least one step that you would like to take in the next week.

For the next four weeks, also resolve to do the following things:

- Consciously give up your personal dopamine kick for a day (e.g., no use of your smartphone on a Sunday, Shabbat, Yawm al-Jumu'ah) or for a week (e.g., no fast food and/or no alcohol).

- Do a physical exercise session for at least thirty minutes twice a week in the fresh air that suits you.

- Perform a morning or evening ritual every day for one week.

Chapter IX

How to Tell If Your Inner Voice
is Helping or Hurting You

*Sometimes the inner voice reminds us of a loving grandparent
who doesn't lecture, but listens compassionately and encourages
us to go our own way. They don't judge; they guide us as only
someone with a lot of life experience can.*

You are now already deeply immersed in the secrets of your
inner voice—which are actually not so secret, just somehow
lost or forgotten. Just like the shepherd Santiago in Paulo
Coelho's book *The Alchemist*, you are on a quest for the
treasure. And like Santiago, you might realize that the
treasure has been with you all along, hidden deep inside you;
it is your inner voice.

As you know by now, I had this experience myself when I found myself in a deep state of exhaustion and ended up in burnout after a divorce and years of professional commitment and increasing inner emptiness. It was only by listening to my inner voice and recognizing the urgency to change something that I found the courage to take a break and finally make a radical life decision: to leave my job of many years, in my own company, in order to save myself.

At the beginning of our short journey together, I prepared you for the fact that you might come across uncomfortable truths about yourself in the course of the book. I mentioned that personal growth often comes with discomfort, but that it's okay to decide for yourself how you want to deal with these realizations in the end. This is still true, so you can continue to sit back, relax, and just read on.

While reading this book, you first dealt with the negative, sabotaging inner voice that often undermines self-confidence in the form of negative beliefs and self-criticism. I explained that this *little voice* arises from cognitive distortions and early experiences and influences us in everyday life.

I then described the good, benevolent inner voice that serves as a source of wisdom and intuition and helps you to make important life decisions. I have shared my personal experiences with you, explaining how my inner voice helped me through difficult times, and I've explained, on a scientific basis, how emotions and bodily sensations contribute to the creation of this inner voice in the brain.

I have tried to show you that listening to your inner voice is very, very important in order to lead an authentic and fulfilling life. I have emphasized that ignoring this voice can lead to wrong decisions, health problems, and great regret at the end of life.

You have learned that people still often ignore their inner voice, even though this can have a negative impact on their well-being. The main reasons for this are a sense of responsibility toward others, the comfort of staying within the familiar zone, and the fear of loss or rejection.

I have given you a whole range of possible behavioral changes that, if you implement them, are guaranteed to enable you to get back in touch with your inner voice.

111

Through techniques such as meditation, exercise in nature, self-reflection, and conscious mindfulness, you can calm your mind and reduce the noise of everyday life.

I would now like to go into more detail about how we can distinguish between the good and the bad inner voice. I would like to provide you with an image that will make it easier for you to distinguish between the two at first glance or *sound*.

Doubt and Fear: The Saboteur's Weapons

The bad, sabotaging inner voice usually sounds very reasonable—almost too reasonable, and that should make you suspicious. It says things like: "Are you sure you can do this? It's better to play it safe and not take any risks. What if you fail and everyone judges you for it? You won't have enough time or energy anyway. It's better to stay where it's comfortable and safe—that's the sensible thing to do!"

This voice pretends to be protective and prudent, but in reality, it stunts progress and growth by constantly sowing doubt and causing you to stay in your comfort zone.

This inner voice also often tends to be dismissive and very strict with you. It says things like: "You're just not good enough. Others would do much better. Why are you even trying if you're going to mess it up anyway? You've failed so many times before—why should it be any different this time? No one will take you seriously if you don't do it perfectly."

This dismissive voice is like a harsh critic who keeps you down and undermines your self-confidence by constantly pointing out supposed mistakes or shortcomings. It makes sure that you constantly doubt yourself and don't dare to break out of your usual patterns.

This inner voice tends to come from the head. It gives you a headache. It comes again and again and its tone is more of a loud, nervous, hectic, sometimes scrambling voice that repeats itself.

Visualizing Your Inner Critic

I thought about what images come to mind for this sabotaging voice and found the following three very fitting:

1. The annoying neighbor

The negative inner voice is like an annoying neighbor who keeps dropping by uninvited to give criticism and advice you never wanted. They show up at your door and say things like: "You're doing it wrong! Believe me, I know, you're going to fail." They interfere in everything, make you feel incompetent, and make you doubt, even though you actually know exactly what you want to do.

2. The strict teacher

The sabotaging inner voice is like an overly strict teacher who never praises you for your progress, but only ever points out your mistakes. No matter how hard you try, they always find something that isn't perfect: "That wasn't good enough! You can't do any better, so you'd better stop trying at all. You'll never amount to anything anyway." This teacher constantly makes you believe that you will never be good enough.

3. The old critic in the stands at a sports stadium

The negative inner voice is like an older, bitter critic sitting in the stands at a game in a stadium and shouting at you from afar that you are never good enough, no matter how hard you fight. He or she (well, in the stadium it's more often a *he*) has never dared to do anything himself and has never been good at your sport, but knows the right insult for every move you make: "Oh man, you're terrible. Completely blind! You can't do anything right. This is going nowhere, just stop. Coach, sub this player out right now, anyone on the bench can do better!" This critic is constantly commenting while you are on the playing field of life.

As a soccer fan who has watched many games live in the stadium in various countries, I am very familiar with the old critic in the stands. He already knows before the game that it's not going to work today and that they're going to lose again anyway. The coach should be sacked and the players can't do anything, even though they are professionals, earn a lot of money, and train every day!

If it suits you better, you can of course also imagine the neighbor or the teacher when you are confronted with your sabotaging inner voice in the future. Or you can have your own image in your head that better suits your individual experiences.

The Quiet Strength of the Benevolent Voice

The good, benevolent inner voice, on the other hand, tends to come from the depths, speaks with a calm and dark voice, feels warm, only wants the best for you, and does not judge or condemn you. It is a wise voice that speaks with a kind of unconditional love and acceptance. Nevertheless, even the good voice is occasionally very insistent and challenging in order to get us out of our comfort zone and to force us a little bit towards our own happiness. Here are three suggestions for images or analogies you could use:

1. The gentle companion

The benevolent inner voice is like a calm, wise companion that always walks by your side. They don't talk loudly and don't constantly interfere, but if you really listen, they give you wise, helpful advice. They know your path and gently support you when you are in doubt or afraid, but they always give you the freedom to make your own decisions.

2. The lighthouse in the fog

The good inner voice is like a lighthouse in the fog—it shines constantly and reliably, showing you the right path, even if you feel lost. It does not force you to follow it, but it is always there to help you navigate safely through stormy times. Its presence is reassuring and gives you the certainty that you are never completely lost as long as you pay attention to it.

3. The loving grandparent

The good inner voice is like a wise, loving grandparent who only ever wishes you the best. They speak calmly and patiently, without putting pressure on you or judging you. This grandparent doesn't care about the little mistakes you make in everyday life, but sees the bigger picture of your life. With their life experience and unwavering faith in you, they remind you that you are valuable just the way you are and that you have the courage to find the right path. They don't want to change you; they just want to encourage you in your own wisdom and give you the peace to listen to your heart. Their words are full of warmth and comfort, like a hug that gives you the feeling that everything will be alright, no matter how difficult the situation seems at the time.

My favorite of the three pictures is the loving grandparent. I myself have fond memories of my two grandmothers and my grandfather who, in the last third or quarter of their lives, no longer took such a narrow view of things and made me, as a grandchild, feel that I was good just the way I am. They had their own educational mission behind them and were much more relaxed and benevolent in their dealings with me.

Choose a picture that suits you. It will help you to more easily assign the voice that is currently speaking within you to the *sabotaging* camp or the *benevolent* camp.

Embracing Your Inner Wisdom

So, ultimately, learning to distinguish between the sabotaging and benevolent inner voices is a critical skill in navigating life's challenges. While the sabotaging voice often stems from fear, self-doubt, and past conditioning, the benevolent voice speaks from a place of wisdom, experience, and deep understanding. By actively recognizing the differences between these voices, you can make conscious decisions that align with your authentic self, rather than being held back by limiting beliefs. The key takeaway is this: the more you practice listening to your inner wisdom—the lighthouse in the fog—the clearer your path will become, allowing you to move forward with confidence and peace.

Exercise 7

The Inner Voice Debate

Goal of the exercise

This exercise is designed to help you consciously engage in a debate between your sabotaging and benevolent inner voices, allowing you to observe how each voice influences your decisions and emotions. By visualizing the old critic in the stadium (or the neighbor or teacher) and the wise grandparent speaking to you, you can identify their distinct impacts. The aim is to actively compare these voices and make a conscious decision about which voice to strengthen, improving your ability to recognize and amplify the benevolent voice while giving less space to the sabotaging one.

Instructions

Step 1. Choose a challenge or decision

Think of a current situation in which you are unsure or facing a decision. It doesn't have to be life-changing; it can also be a more everyday situation that has been on your mind for a while.

Step 2. Let the sabotaging voice speak
Write down what the old critic in the stands says about this challenge or decision. Let him express his doubts, fears, and reservations. Don't hold anything back—allow all the critical thoughts that pop into your head.

Step 3. Let the benevolent voice answer
Now change your perspective and write what the wise grandparent says about this challenge. What encouraging or reassuring thoughts do they have? How would they view the situation? Formulate a clear and compassionate response.

Step 4. Observe the emotional difference
Read through both sections and pay attention to how you feel. Do you feel more tension or insecurity with the sabotaging voice? Do you feel calmer or clearer in your thoughts with the benevolent voice? Make a note of your observations.

Step 5. Make a conscious decision

After you have heard both voices, reflect on which one you would like to prioritize more in this situation. Which voice supports your long-term goals and well-being?

Chapter X

The Wisdom of Looking Back –
Times Our Inner Voice Guided Us Well

In the course of this book, you may have already asked yourself whether and how your inner voice has brought you to where you are in life today. That's good, because reflecting on what your inner voice is capable of is helpful—and can be very powerful. Before we come back to you, let's look at some examples of when people have followed their inner voice and have done very well with it, for themselves and/or others.

History's Courageous Voices: Standing for Change

If you look at world history, literature, or even the world of cinema, there are numerous impressive figures who have followed their inner voice against all odds, taken great steps, and thus brought about significant changes in the lives of many. I am always full of respect and sympathy for people who have taken such steps, often against tough external or internal resistance. Here are a few examples that I personally find very impressive.

In 1955, the African-American Rosa Parks refused to give up her seat on a bus to a white passenger in Montgomery, Alabama. At that time, racial segregation prevailed in the southern states of the USA. African-Americans were systematically discriminated against and had fewer rights than white Americans. There were separate facilities, which were generally much worse for Blacks than for whites. Although she knew this would be a huge challenge for her and her community, Rosa Parks listened to her inner voice that told her it was time to stand up for equality. Her decision sparked the Montgomery bus boycott and became a turning point in the civil rights movement in the USA.

Irena Sendler was a Polish nurse and social worker who rescued around 2,500 Jewish children from the Nazis during the Holocaust or Shoah. Sendler smuggled Jewish children out of the Warsaw ghetto, particularly in 1942 and 1943, provided them with fake identities, and placed them with

Catholic families or in convents. She was arrested by the Gestapo, Nazi Germany's ruthless secret police force, but survived torture and the concentration camp. Her story became known worldwide and she is considered one of the great heroines of the Second World War.

Wangari Maathai was a Kenyan environmental activist and the founder of the Green Belt Movement, which campaigned for reforestation, environmental protection, and women's rights. In the 1970s, Maathai observed the ongoing deforestation and its impact on the environment and living conditions in Kenya. Despite opposition from the government and a lack of funding, she was convinced that reforestation would not only protect the environment but also improve the lives of rural communities. She followed her inner conviction that planting trees was also an act of resistance against poverty and social injustice. To date, her Green Belt Movement has planted over 50 million trees in Kenya and given hundreds of thousands of women the opportunity to earn an income through this work. Wangari Maathai was awarded the Nobel Peace Prize in 2004 and was the first African woman to receive this award.

Rigoberta Menchú is a Guatemalan indigenous human rights activist who fought for the rights of indigenous peoples in Guatemala and Latin America. Menchú, who herself comes from the indigenous K'iche'Maya community, experienced brutal violence and the persecution of her family and community by the Guatemalan military during the civil war in her youth. Despite these atrocities, she followed her conviction that the path to justice lies in the defense of the human rights of the indigenous people. She publicized the abuses through international campaigns and publications. Rigoberta Menchú was awarded the Nobel Peace Prize in 1992 for her commitment to the rights of indigenous peoples and her work helped to raise awareness of the social injustices in Guatemala. Her book *I, Rigoberta Menchú* became a symbolic work for the struggle of indigenous peoples in Latin America.

Malala Yousafzai is a Pakistani activist who, at a young age, began campaigning for the right to education for girls, particularly in the Taliban-controlled region of Swat in northwest Pakistan. Despite threats from the Taliban, who banned girls from attending school, and the danger to her own life, Malala continued to attend school and publicly advocated for the right to education for all girls. She believed that this was the key to freedom and development for girls and women. Her inner conviction was so strong that she continued her mission even after an assassination attempt by the Taliban in 2012. Malala survived the attack and became the world's youngest Nobel Peace Prize winner in 2014. She continued her work for girls' education worldwide and founded the Malala Fund, which campaigns for access to education for girls in crisis regions.

These are real examples of people who have acted from their deepest inner conviction and a clear value system and have thus achieved great positive changes for the lives of many. I deliberately chose examples exclusively from women be-cause the resistance they had to overcome in many of the world's more male-dominated societies makes what they achieved even more impressive to me.

Listening to Convictions in Times of Doubt

I also admire stories of people who have listened to their inner voice on the basis of vague information, without real evidence and against generally prevailing opinions or world views, and have thus achieved major changes for the whole of humanity. Here are a few examples.

Galileo Galilei was one of the first scientists to publicly support the Copernican world view (the sun as the center of the solar system) from the early 1600s in what is now Italy. At that time, however, the geocentric world view prevailed, which stated that the Earth was the center of the universe, which belief was also defended by the Catholic Church as a dogmatic truth. Despite the strong religious and scientific opposition, Galileo was convinced of the correctness of the heliocentric model, based on his own observations with the telescope. He defended his findings, even when he was threatened for doing so. Galileo was accused of heresy by the church and placed under house arrest. It was not until centuries later that his work was recognized as revolutionary, and he is now considered one of the founders of modern astronomy and physics.

Charles Darwin was a British naturalist who developed the theory of natural selection in the 19th century. Darwin followed his conviction that all species emerged from common ancestors through a slow, natural selection process. This was at odds with the prevailing religious and scientific beliefs about creation at the time. Although Darwin's theory caused much controversy, it was later recognized as one of the most fundamental theories in biology. It laid the foundation for the modern understanding of evolution and genetic diversity.

The Hungarian doctor Ignaz Semmelweis worked as an obstetrician in a hospital in Vienna (Austria) in the mid-19th century. He observed that women often died of puerperal fever after giving birth and became convinced that the disease was spread by a lack of hygiene--in particular by doctors who went straight from seeing corpses to assisting births without washing their hands. Although the germ theory of infection was not yet recognized at the time, Semmelweis was convinced that washing hands with chlorinated solutions could prevent the spread of the disease. His measure dramatically reduced the mortality rate, but his ideas were rejected by the medical community of his time as there was no scientific evidence of germs or bacteria. It wasn't until decades later, with the work of Louis Pasteur and others, that the germ theory was proven and Semmelweis' beliefs were recognized.

The German meteorologist and geoscientist Alfred Wegener put forward the theory of continental drift at the beginning of the 20th century. Wegener was convinced that the continents once formed a supercontinent and moved apart over time. Despite the opposition of the geologists of his time, who rejected his theory because he could not provide a convincing mechanism for the movement of the continents, he stuck to his idea. It was not until decades after Wegener's death that his theory was confirmed and formed the basis of today's plate tectonics, which is considered revolutionary for the understanding of geology and the history of the earth.

Barry Marshall, an Australian physician, together with Robin Warren, discovered the bacterium *Helicobacter pylori* as the main cause of stomach ulcers. Marshall was convinced that stomach ulcers were not caused by stress or stomach acid alone, as was widely believed at the time, but by a bacterium. As his theory was met with skepticism, he decided to test the bacterium on himself by deliberately infecting himself with it. Marshall's self-experiment and his research led to the revolutionary realization that bacteria are the main cause of stomach ulcers, which drastically improved treatment options. He was awarded the Nobel Prize for Medicine in 2005.

It's impressive what the inner voice can drive people to do, isn't it?

However, there are many more *ordinary* examples, including my own, of people who listened to their inner voice and have *simply* been able to lead a more fulfilling life.

Personal Treasures: Following the Call for Authenticity

The young Andalusian shepherd Santiago in Paulo Coelho's *The Alchemist* (I know I am repeating myself here, but I really liked the book) is driven by a recurring dream to find a hidden treasure in the pyramids of Egypt. Santiago senses deep within himself that this dream is no coincidence, but a message from his inner voice telling him to leave his comfortable life behind and go in search of his personal treasure. Despite the uncertainty and the obstacles he encounters on his journey, he unwaveringly follows this inner conviction. On his long journey, Santiago learns a lot about himself, life, and the universe. He discovers that the real treasure is not the material goods at the end of his journey, but the wisdom and self-knowledge he gains along the way.

Elizabeth Gilbert describes in her memoir *Eat, Pray, Love* (book/film) how, after a difficult divorce, she follows her inner voice, which tells her that she needs to experience something new and break away from societal expectations. Liz leaves her old life behind and embarks on a journey to Italy, India, and Bali to explore self-discovery, spirituality, and love. This journey changes her life profoundly. She not only finds the answers she was looking for, but also the strength to live her life authentically and free from external expectations.

Christopher McCandless, also known as *Alexander Supertramp*, was a young man from the USA who, after graduating from college, decided to break away from conventional society and material values in order to live a simple and free life in the wilderness. McCandless followed his inner conviction that true happiness lies in freedom and connection to nature. He refused his parents' financial inheritance to travel across North America, eventually settling in the wilderness of Alaska. His life was immortalized in the book and film *Into the Wild*. McCandless found fulfillment through his radical lifestyle, but died tragically in the wilderness. His story serves as both a warning and an inspiration. It encourages people to think about fundamental questions in life like: What really makes us happy? How do we find a balance between personal freedom and responsibility? What role does nature play in our lives? Despite the tragic ending, McCandless's quest for an authentic life inspires many people to question their own values and search for deeper meaning.

I also find Forrest Gump, the main character of the movie and book of the same name, to be very inspiring. For me, he is an example of how smart life decisions and success do not necessarily have to depend on strong cognitive abilities or a high intelligence quotient. Forrest makes many of his decisions based on his simple, authentic sense of what is right. He goes his own way without much questioning and without worrying about the opinions of others. Although Forrest's life is filled with many challenges, he experiences a number of remarkable successes and ends up leading a fulfilling life. His story shows that listening to your heart and living in the here and now can lead to a happy and meaningful life, even if you don't conform to society's *normal* expectations.

As a book author, I am of course particularly fascinated by J.K. Rowling, who became world-famous thanks to the Harry Potter series. She followed her inner voice, which told her that she had to put her fantasy world about a young wizard on paper, even though she was going through a difficult phase in her life. Despite financial hardship and numerous publishers rejecting her manuscript, Rowling held on to her dream of telling the story she felt deep down was important. The publication of the Harry Potter books changed her life completely. The books became a global success and Rowling inspired many people to follow their own creativity and inner voice.

Why is it helpful to look at these historical figures and their stories when reflecting on your own inner voice? These individuals—whether activists, scientists, or thinkers—faced immense external challenges, yet chose to trust their inner convictions even when the world around them doubted or resisted them. Their stories show us that intuition, when deeply connected to core values and beliefs, can lead to groundbreaking changes not just for the individual, but for society as a whole. In hindsight, it is obvious that their inner voice was the right voice to follow. Imagine being in the situation of these individuals when everything and everybody is against you.

By examining the choices they made, often in the face of uncertainty or opposition, we can gain a better understanding of how our inner voice operates. It's not about comparing our lives to theirs, but about recognizing that our inner voice—no matter how small or insignificant it may seem—can have a profound impact on the direction we choose to take. Their courage in listening to themselves reminds us that, even in our daily lives, tuning in to our intuition can guide us toward fulfilling and authentic decisions, even when it feels risky or challenges the usual path.

Ordinary People, Extraordinary Decisions

I personally know several striking examples from my circle of acquaintances where the inner voice has done remarkable work. In recent years, I've met two men who pulled the ripcord shortly (and I mean very shortly) before their own wedding and called everything off. This crass and courageous move leaves a lot of collateral damage in its wake, at least for the almost-future bride, the families, and all the guests who have already been invited. Not to mention the weight of guilt the *runaway groom* had to manage on his own. Both men have become very happy with their new partners—and as far as I know, so have the almost-brides.

As an entrepreneur myself and having met many, many other entrepreneurs—large and small, successful and less successful—over the years, I learned that there were also quite a few among them who simply had to start their own business because their inner voice kept telling them to. Some already had this intuition as a child or teenager. Many of them left the security of a high-paying job and entered the uncertainty that comes with founding a start-up. From the outside, you often only see success when it works. However, hardly anyone realizes that the road to success can be extremely exhausting, full of privation, frustrating, and lonely.

Life's Turning Points: My Own Inner Voice Experience

I'm grateful to realize that my inner voice served as a reliable guide through the key turning points in my life—until, midway through, I nearly lost touch with it completely. It had to wake me up again with a loud cry on that ominous late summer weekend, just before I turned fifty.

Looking back, I realize I had a potentially life-changing experience just a few months shy of my twenty-first birthday. On an early Sunday evening in the summer (I remember it quite clearly, that day was the final of the 1994 soccer world cup in the USA, when Brazil only won against Italy in a penalty shoot-out), I ended an almost five-year relationship with my girlfriend. I only realized the importance of this many years later. I didn't end it because the relationship was so terrible or even toxic. No, we got along well, liked each other very much, had a mutual circle of friends, I went in and out of her parents' house, and I even went on a summer vacation with her and her parents. Yet I wasn't happy anymore and knew deep down that it wasn't the relationship I wanted and it never would be again. We were like brother and sister, but no longer the romantic, passionate couple that you actually want to be (and should be) at this stage of your life. I spent the entire Sunday working at my side job at the horse race-track, taking betting slips and processing them through the so-called totalizator, which automatically recorded and handled the wagers. All day long, my inner voice spoke to me in a calm and friendly voice and told me what I already knew: "You're unhappy. It's better for you to break up." However, the other voice inside me kept replying with various objections such as: "You can't do this to her! She'll be completely

137

blindsided and heartbroken. What will your mutual friends think of you? The whole friend group will fall apart. And her parents—they'll be so disappointed in you ..." and so on. In hindsight, this step was pivotal for me, as it marked the first time I made a truly far-reaching decision completely on my own, trusting it would serve my life and well-being in the best way possible. I did this against a lot of supposed resistance and at the cost of *ruining everything*. When my shift at the racecourse was over, I went straight to her and told her to her face. This was a very, very difficult walk, but afterwards, a load was off my mind. All my worries were not confirmed. Our friends remained our friends, at least the *right* ones. And we are actually still good friends today, and many years later I was even allowed to become her son's godfather. This experience often sustained me later in life, because I knew that there was an inner voice that only wanted the best for me.

Reflecting on Your Own Journey: Your Inner Voice in Action

Now I would like to invite you to reflect on your life. When has your inner voice guided you in the past? What kind of situation was it? And what positive changes did it bring about in your life?

Exercise 8

Reflecting on When Your Inner Voice Led You to Good Choices

Goal of the exercise

This exercise is designed to help you to consciously perceive the positive experiences in your life that have come about by listening to your inner voice. It should give you a good feeling and remind you that your intuition has often helped you—and that it can continue to show you the way to beautiful and fulfilling moments.

Instructions

Step 1. Record positive decisions and experiences

- Think of three to five positive decisions or moments in your life when you listened to your inner voice. These can be major life decisions or small, everyday choices—the key is the positive impact they've had.

- Examples: Perhaps you spontaneously decided to go on a trip that gave you unforgettable experiences, or you trusted a new friendship that enriched your life.

Step 2. Reflect on feelings and positive effects
Make a note of how it felt in those moments when you listened to your inner voice.

- How did your inner voice feel? Was it quiet but firm? Did you feel a sense of clarity or calm?

- What positive changes or experiences have resulted from this? How have you benefited from it?

- Remember how satisfied you felt after making this decision and how it has helped you move forward.

Step 3. Smile at the beautiful memories

- Close your eyes for a moment and think of these beautiful memories.

- Allow yourself to relive the good feeling and the joy that these decisions brought into your life.

- Feel the smile that spreads across your face as you remember this time in your life.

Step 4. Build trust for the future

Finally, write down a sentence that reminds you to listen more to your inner voice in future. For example:

- "My inner voice has already brought me so many wonderful experiences—I trust that it will continue to guide me well."

  or

- "When I listen to my inner voice, I often find the way to moments that make me happy."

Chapter XI

Head, Heart, or Gut:
How We Process Our Inner Voice

I already explained to you in chapter V that the inner voice is likely a combination of rational thinking, emotional processing, and bodily sensations. In other words, you could say: head (rational thinking), heart (emotions), and gut (bodily sensations). You're probably familiar with the simplified categorization of some people as head-, heart-, or gut-oriented individuals. You can also call them thinkers, feelers, and gut thinkers.

These categories can also occur in combination, and you could find yourself in all three categories. If I had to categorize myself, I'd say I'm first a head-oriented person, then gut, and lastly heart. I see this as both a strength and a weakness. It's a strength because I keep a cool head even in

143

the most difficult situations and am often perceived by those around me as the rock in the surf. It's also a weakness, because I find it more difficult to be sensitive to the emotional level in interpersonal relationships and to always consciously feel and show my own feelings.

Now I've asked myself whether it makes a difference in how a person perceives their inner voice depending on which category they fall into. To get straight to the point, the answer is: Yes, it does.

I have already told you that, in addition to my own very significant experiences with the inner voice, I have also read literature and studies on the subject. While reading them, a certain pattern emerged for me that I would like to share.

My thesis that there are head people, heart people, and gut people who perceive their inner voice in very different ways and accordingly make decisions differently is confirmed when you combine the approaches and theories of various authors and researchers. In my opinion, these concepts offer valuable insights into the way people experience their intuition and inner voice— be it through quick action, deep emotional reflection, or rational thought.

The Thinkers: Rational Decision-Making Through the Head

Let's start with Daniel Kahneman, who I have already told you about. He describes the two systems of human thinking in his book *Thinking, Fast and Slow*. The distinction between head and gut people fits perfectly here. Kahneman talks about System 1, which works quickly, intuitively and unconsciously—exactly what we see in gut thinkers who listen to their inner voice, which reacts quickly and often instinctively. In contrast to this is System 2, which acts slowly, analytically and consciously—here we recognize the thinkers who make decisions methodically and thoughtfully. However, Kahneman clearly shows that both systems are important and should complement each other. After all, the right mix of intuitive and analytical thinking often leads to the best decisions.

Feelers and Gut Thinkers: Acting on Emotion and Instinct

Gerd Gigerenzer also argues along these lines in *Gut Feelings* when he emphasizes the importance of gut feeling. He is convinced that intuitive and spontaneous decisions are often the better ones, as they are based on experience and quick

THE SECRET TO DOING THE RIGHT THING

heuristics. This is particularly relevant for gut instincts—they rely on simple decision-making rules and can often act successfully as a result. Gigerenzer's work emphasizes that we can trust our intuition, because we often unconsciously sense what is right.

In *Little Voice Mastery*, Blair Singer talks about the inner voice that often challenges us. It can appear as a critical dialogue, full of self-doubt and insecurities. Head people could be particularly affected here, as they are often caught up in their thinking and allow themselves to be influenced by rational, but also negative, self-talk. On the other hand, heart people and gut people may be less affected by these critical inner voices, as they tend to make their decisions intuitively or emotionally and therefore often experience more positive inner guidance.

Another interesting approach comes from Antonio Damasio with his somatic marker hypothesis. Damasio shows that emotions and physical sensations often unconsciously influence our decisions. Gut thinkers feel these signals particularly strongly, whether as a feeling in their stomach or as another physical reaction that guides them without them consciously realizing it. Head people, on the other hand, may try to ignore these physical signals and rely on rational reasoning instead, while heart people or feelers allow their emotions to play a stronger role in their decisions and are therefore more deeply connected to their feelings.

In *Radical Acceptance,* Tara Brach emphasizes the importance of emotional intelligence and the ability to acknowledge and accept feelings. For people of heart, this is of central importance—their inner voice is guided by their emotions. By learning to accept their feelings and give them space, they can make decisions that are in line with their emotional feelings. For feelers, it's about establishing a deep connection to their emotional world and using it as a compass for their actions.

Daniel Goleman also emphasizes the role of emotions and their conscious perception in *Emotional Intelligence.* According to Goleman, people of heart are those who listen to their emotions in particular and use them to guide their decisions. They have a high level of emotional intelligence, which helps them to understand and shape interpersonal relationships. In contrast, thinkers tend to regulate or rationalize their emotions so as not to let them influence their decisions too much.

And finally, we have Clarissa Pinkola Estés, who talks about returning to our instinctive nature in *Women Who Run with the Wolves*. Here we see the gut people who are most closely connected to their inner voice and instincts. They rely on unconscious reactions that are deeply rooted in us and often point the direct way to the right decisions. Especially for women, who in our society have often been brought up to suppress their inner impulses, this return to their instinctive nature is an important step towards self-liberation and the rediscovery of their own inner wisdom.

To me, these different perspectives from other authors on the phenomenon of the inner voice suggest that people perceive their inner voice in different ways—whether as intuitive impulses, emotional signals, or rational self-talk. I would like to invite you to recognize which *type* you are and how the inner voice can be better used and strengthened in your life.

How Men and Women Experience Their Inner Voice Differently

Incidentally, I am also convinced that there are sometimes significant differences between the sexes in this respect. There is even scientific and psychological evidence that men and women perceive and express their inner voice differently, which is mainly due to biological and cultural differences. Women tend to perceive their inner voice more through emotional and interpersonal intuition, while men tend to rely more on rational and analytical processes. However, I don't want to go into the topic of *men and women* any further at this point, as it would involve too many facets. I am therefore considering writing my own book on the subject of men and women, which goes beyond the perception of the inner voice, as I myself find it simultaneously so difficult and fascinating how the sexes attract each other and yet often find it so difficult to understand each other. Please let me know by email to *books@henrykdeter.com* whether you would be interested in this or which aspects you would find interesting.

Despite the differences in whether and how men and women perceive their inner voice, the results are often similar. This became clear to me while reading *The Top 5 Regrets of the*

Dying, which I mentioned earlier: both men and women regret, at the end of their lives, not having listened to their inner voice enough.

Exercise 9

What type are you?

Goal of the exercise

This exercise is designed to help you get a clearer picture of whether you are more of a head person, a heart person, or a gut person. It makes you aware of how you make your decisions and helps you to specifically recognize and strengthen your inner voice—depending on how you act intuitively.

Instructions

Step 1. Thinking back to past decisions

- Take a moment to think about three important decisions you have made in your life.
- These decisions can come from different areas, e.g., career, relationships, or personal goals.

- Write them down in bullet points to make yourself aware of them.

Step 2. Analyze the basis for the decision

For each of these three decisions, answer the following questions:

- Did you make the decision primarily analytically and logically?
  - o If so, this could be an indication that you are a thinker.
- Was your decision strongly guided by your feelings and emotions?
  - o Then you probably tend to be a feeler.
- Did you mainly listen to your gut feeling or intuition without giving it much thought?
  - o Then this indicates that you are a gut thinker.

Step 3. Observe physical reactions

Think back to a decision that was particularly important to you and remember what was going on in your body:

- Were you tense, thinking and weighing things up a lot?
  - o A sign for the head person.

- Did you feel a strong sensation in your chest or heart?
  - o This could indicate the heart person.
- Did you have a clear gut feeling that pushed you in one direction or another?
  - o An indication of the gut person.

Step 4. Discover your tendency

Now take a look at the answers to your questions. In most cases, did you act rationally and analytically, react emotionally, or trust your intuition?

- If you have mostly thought and analyzed, then you are probably a head person.
- If you let your feelings guide you, you are more likely to be a person of the heart.
- If your gut feeling points you in the right direction, you are a gut thinker.

Step 5. Conscious experimentation

In the next few days or weeks, when you are faced with a decision, pause and consciously ask yourself:

- How does that make me feel?
- Do I follow my head, my heart, or my gut?
- Make a note of your observations to recognize which aspect of the inner voice is strongest for you.

Chapter XII

Your Next Big Move

If you've read this far, then your inner voice has probably already been speaking to you a few times. Perhaps your mind has regularly switched on and your thoughts have wandered while reading, thinking about something very important in your life that has been bothering you for some time and causing you stress. Or you had that feeling in the pit of your stomach, a rumbling, a pressure, perhaps heartburn, or even a warm and cozy feeling. Perhaps your emotional world has revealed itself, you've got goose bumps, a smile has flitted across your face, or you've even shed a few tears.

Now is the perfect moment to take a closer, more concrete look at your life. I'd like to help guide you through this with a clear structure. Take some dedicated time to work through the following final exercise.

Exercise 10

The Wisdom of Your Inner Voice—
What Should I Change in My Life?

Goal of the exercise

This exercise helps you to consciously question your inner voice and use it as a guide to find out what needs to be changed in your life. By reflecting on the four areas of life and questioning your inner wisdom directly, you can recognize what changes are necessary to lead a more fulfilling life and avoid regrets later on. By involving your future self, you will gain a deeper perspective on the consequences of your decisions today.

Instructions

Step 1. Create a calm connection to your inner voice

- Before you start, take a moment to calm down and consciously connect with your inner voice. Sit in a quiet place, close your eyes, and take a few deep breaths in and out. Leave everyday life and all external influences behind you for a moment.

- Visualize that your inner voice is by your side like a friendly, wise companion—ready to help you find clarity. Think of the wise, loving grandparent if you liked this image.

Step 2. Reflect on areas of your life

Now consciously consider the four important areas of life and ask yourself for each one:

- **Work**: What does my inner voice say about my professional situation? Do I feel fulfilled and on the right path? Or are there aspects that have been giving me the feeling for some time that I should change something?

- **Relationship**: What does my inner voice tell me about my partnership or my love life? Do I feel loved, respected, and valued? Do I see my own needs fulfilled? Is there something that I have felt for a long time but have ignored until now?

- **Family & Friends**: How are my relationships with my family and friends? Which relationships feel good to me, and which ones weigh me down? Have I missed opportunities to connect with people, or are there important conversations that need to be had?

- **Me** (personal well-being, health, self-development): What is my inner voice telling me about the way I look after myself? Do I have enough space for my health, my dreams, and my personal development? Am I allowing external obligations to overshadow my inner fulfillment?

Step 3. Listen to the quiet voices

- For each area of your life, write down in bullet points what your inner voice is telling you. Pay particular attention to quiet, subliminal hints—as you know, the inner voice is not loud, but gentle and careful.

- What areas immediately spring to mind when you think of change?

- Which aspects have you perhaps been putting off or ignoring for a long time, even though your inner voice has often pointed them out to you?

Step 4. Ask specific questions

Ask yourself the following questions for each area of your life and consciously listen to yourself:

- What should change in order to live a more fulfilling life in this area?
- What do I already feel now that could lead me to regret in the future if I don't change it?
- What could I do today to avoid this regret and increase my satisfaction?

Step 5. Write down the answers of your inner voice

Write down everything that comes to mind without evaluating or analyzing it. Let your inner voice speak freely. It knows what is good for you, even if you don't have a solution ready yet.

Make a note for each area of life:

- What needs to change?
- Why is this change important?
- How would your life feel if this change took place?

Step 6. Ask your future self for advice

Picture yourself toward the end of your life—say, at ninety years old—looking back on everything you've done. Imagine what your older, wiser self would advise you to do right now. Ask your future self:

- What do you wish you had done differently so that you could have lived the life you really wanted?

- Are there relationships you would have cultivated differently, dreams you would have pursued sooner, or decisions you should have made earlier?

- Write down these insights. What does your future self want to tell you today?

Step 7. Summarize your findings

Now summarize the most important points that your inner voice and your future self have revealed to you:

- What are the most urgent changes?

- Which areas are already good, but could be even more fulfilling?

- Where is the risk that you will regret something at the end of your life if nothing changes?

Chapter XIII

The Final Step: Trusting and Acting on Your Inner Voice

A journey of a thousand miles begins with a single step.
Lao Tzu, Chinese philosopher, founder of Taoism,
probably 6th century BC

Celebrating Your Journey: Trusting What You've Learned

So, you've almost finished reading this book. Thank you for your trust! And congratulations! You have engaged with your inner voice! If you have done this seriously and consistently, followed my recommendations, and practiced the exercises for a few weeks, then you have heard your inner voice. I mean the benevolent one, the grandparent, not the critical and annoying one. It's still there, but you pay less attention to it than before.

It may be that your inner voice is signaling a lot of approval for the way you are leading your life. That it confirms that you agree with how your partnership, family, friendships, and career have developed recently. And that you feel good in your own skin, physically and mentally. That you are on the right path to not being one of those who will eventually leave this world with one of *the top five regrets of the dying* (or other essential regrets that were not on that list).

If that's the case, great! Keep living your best life. Trust yourself and your inner voice. Be aware that the changes that will happen in your environment and in yourself in the future (yes, that's certain to happen, I'm sorry) will require you to keep sharpening your compass and checking whether you're still on course.

However, it may also be (and this is actually quite likely) that you have heard or sensed something that requires one or even several changes in your life if you trust your inner voice and follow it (I have explained why you should definitely do this). Now you are right to ask me: What do I do with these insights?

Take the First Step Toward Change

I know that sounds too simple, but the truth is: do it! Do it! Do it! Consciously take the first step out of your comfort zone and tackle the change you already feel inside you. Stop thinking about it endlessly and looking for excuses, but get into action. Yes, it can be difficult. Yes, it can hurt, both for you and for other people in your immediate environment. But trust me: it's the best thing for you. I estimate the probability is at least 99% that it won't be as bad as you're currently imagining. Our brains tend to overestimate the possible negative effects of our actions and minimize the opportunities they offer. Trust your inner voice; it's right. Start with the first step, then more steps will occur and will feel natural as you follow your inner voice.

The Power of Patience

Maybe you're now saying: "Well, thank you very much. Now I'm sitting here with this new, uncomfortable realization and I'm not even ready to change the course of my life, let alone turn the tide completely. No! I am not sufficiently prepared to implement these changes now." If you say all that, then I have excellent news for you: that's perfectly okay. Yes, you read that right: it's totally fine. Even if it sounds like a contradiction to what I've just told you, it's a valid option not to change anything for the time being. Everything stays as it is. I'll explain why. I only came to this realization myself a few years ago and it was a real eye-opener for me. I had a conversation with a friend, an entrepreneur like me, and a quite successful one at that. As we often do, we were talking about challenges with our dear employees. He had a leading employee who was simply not performing. Objectively, there was every reason not to keep him on but it is always difficult and unpleasant for entrepreneurs to make such decisions, as human destinies are potentially always involved. It also happens that important projects are currently underway or other circumstances make it very difficult to do without this employee from one day to the next. This often leads to the entrepreneur postponing the decision, and thinking and probably talking about this employee every day. Since the employer is practical, he looks for reasons to view the employee favorably, allowing him to avoid making the difficult decision to terminate his employment. Then the employee makes another mistake and the boss is on the verge of firing the employee on the spot, again. So, it goes back and forth and back and forth. This can severely affect productivity, as it costs time. Above all, it costs an incredible amount of energy and nerves. So, my friend said to me: "I've already made my decision: I'm going to part ways with this employee. That's for sure. Now I don't need to think about it anymore, I just need to decide when and how best to implement this decision. It doesn't have to be immediately." If you're now saying: "Huh? This approach is obvious, why are you making such a fuss about it now?" This approach of decoupling the implementation of the decision from the decision-making process was actually new to me at the time. I thought, if I have a clear insight, then I have to put it into practice in both business and other areas of my life. Yet that's not the case. No one said that making and implementing a decision had to follow each other immediately. I've been applying this ever since, and it works really well for me because it gives me significantly more peace of mind. I no longer have to constantly reopen the same old issues in my mind and endlessly go around in circles.

Trust Your Subconscious

Why am I telling you this? Because you have the option to do the same: perhaps the insight you have recently gained about your life while reading this book is quite big. The

167

thought of putting it into practice intimidates you. Then just give yourself some time. Now that you have come to this realization, it will work in your subconscious all by itself, whether you like it or not. You have already taken the first step towards implementing it. When you are ready, you will take the next concrete steps to implement it. You are probably already doing it, because your subconscious is already influencing your actions without you always realizing it.

Baby Steps, Big Impact

If you choose the last option, please only do me one favor: don't question your newfound knowledge! Your inner voice has spoken to you and I am personally convinced that it only wants the best for you. Trust it. Focus now only on implementation. Perhaps you talk to very close confidants about the decision you have now made for your life. Perhaps you make a plan as to when and with which steps you want to start and follow through with the implementation. Find your own way to follow your inner voice. It doesn't have to entail a big leap into the deep end like I did when I took a break from my own company and never returned. Baby steps are often perhaps even the better tactic. Oh, and do you know who's best to consult on the right steps to take? Your inner voice. I'm 100% sure it will have some very benevolent suggestions for you.

Like a good grandparent sitting by the fireplace
and sharing the stories of life,
the benevolent inner voice speaks
with wisdom and without haste.
It knows that everything will find its way
if you only trust in it.

My Book Recommendations

The following books, listed in alphabetical order, are some examples of works that invite you to reflect on your own life and discover your inner voice through symbolic stories, spiritual questions, and the search for your own path.

Jonathan Livingston Seagull by Richard Bach
Siddhartha by Hermann Hesse
The Cafe on the Edge of the World by John Strelecky
The Dolphin: Story of a Dreamer by Sergio Bambaren
The Little Prince by Antoine de Saint-Exupéry

I have also learned a lot from several non-fiction books and received valuable impulses. The following books offer approaches for how to connect with the inner voice, whether through meditation, self-reflection, or releasing external expectations. They help one to recognize the inner wisdom that speaks through thoughts, emotions, and physical sensations, and encourage you to follow this inner compass to lead a more fulfilling life.

Descartes' Error: Emotion, Reason, and the Human Brain by
Antonio R. Damasio
Full Catastrophe Living by Jon Kabat-Zinn
How to Stop Worrying and Start Living by Dale Carnegie
Life Worth Living: A Guide to What Matters Most
by Miroslav Volf, Matthew Croasmun
and Ryan McAnnally-Linz
The Courage to Be Disliked by Ichiro Kishimi
and Fumitake Koga

Of course, there are countless wonderful books that offer valuable insights on living a more fulfilling life.

I sincerely hope that this book has now become one of those for you.

I'd love to hear about your experience—please feel free to share your feedback with me at *books@henrykdeter.com*.

Made in United States
Cleveland, OH
04 January 2025

13092317R00105